Writing 30

By Robert Creeley

Robert Creeley

CONTEXTS OF POETRY:
*   INTERVIEWS 1961-1971*

edited by Donald Allen

Four Seasons Foundation
Bolinas: 1973

I have a curious feeling about the material here collected. The reflection, so to speak, which these interviews make possible for me, substantiates a sense of *I* that the other 'I' of my nature rarely was aware of in actual writing. The questioners of course had their own preoccupations and so Black Mountain College, for one instance, seems almost a myth as it comes into the divers texts again and again. What is interesting, I think, is that which one *does* say, over and over, without being really aware of it. For better or for worse, these insistences must be the measure of one's acts.

The interviews took place in a variety of circumstances. In some cases the interviewers were particular friends who had come to our house, making the whole occasion happily relaxed and informal. Charles Tomlinson and Lewis MacAdams were generously of this company. Linda Wagner's contribution, on the other hand, was arranged by her sending written questions which I then answered using a tape recorder, leaving the incredible labor of transcribing it all to her. The talking I did at the Vancouver Poetry Conference in company with Allen Ginsberg was part of a so-called class meeting and again the transcription was done by a friend and then student, George Butterick. John Sinclair--a man I liked and respected on the instant--in company with Robin Eichele managed to get me while we

were both enjoying a timeout at a friend's
house during the Berkeley Poetry Conference.
David Ossman's was done at WBAI's studio in
New York and did feel intimidating and rushed,
no doubt simply that it is the first. In contrast the next to last interview consists of
answers written by me to a list of questions
which the *New American Review* was using as
basis for a symposium called "The Writer's
Situation." The two remaining were done by
active students at Indiana University and the
University of New Mexico, people who have always been good news. The time between the first
and the last is just about ten years.

    Finally I should like to thank all those I
have mentioned, just that without them this
book would not exist.

                       R.C.

Bolinas, California
September 14, 1972

CONTENTS

CONTEXTS OF POETRY

DAVID OSSMAN: INTERVIEW
WITH ROBERT CREELEY

Creeley squeezed in this interview on the Saturday morning in May, 1961, that he was to leave New York, having only recently returned to the States from Guatemala.

Ossman: What was it about the atmosphere at Black Mountain College that so influenced the students?

Creeley: At the time I was there, the college was in very straitened circumstances and had a great deal of difficulty in maintaining its operation, so that I think everyone present felt a curiously useful desperation. It finally proved the end of the college, of course, but I think we all felt a seriousness and an openness of form and intention that was extremely useful to all concerned. The students, I suppose, had a more difficult time than the faculty, although the faculty seems to have had troubles enough, but we were very much concerned with the problems of experimental education and what could be done now. We wanted a kind of teaching that usually depended upon actually being involved in the materials that were being used. So that, for example, in painting or writing, we had people who were painters or writers, as opposed to those who might be more theoretically involved.
    Now how that relates to poetry is a more diffuse question. At first there was the hope

to publicize the college, and to make people
aware that it was continuing, by publishing a
magazine. This was, we thought, the most quick
and simple manner of telling people we were
still alive.

Ossman: When did the *Black Mountain Review*
start, actually?

Creeley: 1954-55, about. I was still in Mallorca, and had been publishing books under the
name of the Divers Press, when Charles Olson,
who was my very good friend although curiously
I'd never met him, suggested I start a magazine, because we happily had the use of cheap
printing and also because, through correspondence, I had access to a good many people who
were very active. And too, we had Cid Corman's
Origin to build on, in a sense. So that was
the beginning of the *Black Mountain Review*.
Shortly after the first issue I went to teach
at Black Mountain, and then I left briefly,
and then came back again.
    I have a little hesitation about the ques-
tion of "schools." I was reading recently at
Goddard College and met the reaction I thought
reasonable: "is Donald Allen's anthology simply another instance of a group which is going
to prove another exclusion for younger people
now trying to find a means and a way in their
own terms of poetry?"
    So I almost would like--not to bury Black
Mountain, because it probably gave me more coherence than I otherwise would have had, certainly that, but I don't like to feel that it's
any exclusion, or any ultimate purpose or form
or *via* that's finally been settled upon once
and for all. We had exceptional students. I
was thinking of Edward Dorn and of Mike Rumaker, specifically those two men, who have consequently proved all that anyone ever hoped of
them. There were many others of that kind--
all the students had that quality of openness
and self-determination.

Ossman: Both students and teachers at Black Mountain seem to write poetry which differs considerably in style from one to the other . . .

Creeley: I think what did happen then, and what continues to happen among these people to join us all together, is this: a very conscious concern with the manner of a poem, with the form of a poem, so that we are, in that way, freed from any solution unparticular or *not* particular to ourselves. Olson, I believe, was a decisive influence upon me as a writer, because he taught me how to write. Not how to write poems that he wrote, but how to write poems that I write. This is a very curious and very specific difference.
    I think of Paul Blackburn, he was really the first poet I ever knew, and I remember arriving in New York in a pretty hysterical fashion--we were about to take one of those boats --and Paul and I spent two and a half days and nights simply talking about *how do you write a poem?* We'd come, very respectfully, from Pound's influence. Pound, again, is back of all this, as is William Carlos Williams. We all had to find the character of our own intelligence, I suppose it would be, our own minds, the terms of our own living, and we did it by this preoccupation with *how is the poem to be put on the page*. Not "how do we feel generally" --are we good people or bad people--but how shall we actually speak to other people in this medium in a way that's not exclusively personal, but in a way that is our own determination.

Ossman: Certainly this whole group of poets has a profound concern for form, and Olson has written a good deal on the subject. How do you feel about the "beat" poets, and other, younger, writers who seem less concerned with matters of form?

Creeley: Let me not try to claim Allen Ginsberg for my side, because he's there anyhow.

I think I'm on his side certainly. Now Allen
made some comments about Whitman's line in a
note on a record of his reading of *Howl and
Other Poems*. He is a conscious writer. I
mean by that, that he is aware of the technical problems of putting words on a page in a
consequent or coherent manner. He specifically seems to be intent on handling this long
line that Whitman developed in a manner, again,
specific to the content that Allen is involved
with.

You see, we're all of us, so to speak, somebody. We all of us have a specific emotional
issue or term of contact in our lives, so that,
in one sense, when someone says, "There's nothing to say," there's almost an impossible
amount of things to say from this basic position. In Allen's terms, he comes, of course,
from an environment that gives him the use of
a kind of litany or ritualistic, chantlike
quality of speaking. He also comes from an
urbanism. Allen is specific to a history of
the growth of a world, I suppose, so that's
something he's got to say.

Ossman: Most of the Black Mountain poets have,
generally, a short, fragmented line and many
cast this into a highly structured phrase. In
turning from *The Whip* to *The Form of Women*, you
developed a more lyrical line. I might add
that it's curious that some of your poems, with
their wry sense of humor, take on the characteristics of a macabre light verse . . .

Creeley: Well, that's a New England temper
you must remember. When things are really impossible, you start laughing--not weakly, the
louder the better. In the earlier poems you
mention, the emotional terms are very difficult.
The poems come from a context that was difficult
to live in, and so I wanted the line to be used
to register that kind of problem, or that kind
of content. Elsewhere I remember I did say
that "Form is never more than an extension of

content," and by that I meant that the thing
to be said will, in that way, determine how it
will be said. So that if you're saying, "Go
light the fire," "fire" in that registration
will have one kind of emphasis, and if you start
screaming, "Fire! Fire!" of course that will
have another. In other words, the content of
what is semantically involved will very much
function in how the statement of it occurs.
Now the truncated line, or the short, seeming-
ly broken line I was using in my first poems,
comes from the somewhat broken emotions that
were involved in them. Now, as I begin to relax, as I not so much grow older, but more
settled, more at ease in my world, the line
can not so much grow softer, but can become,
as you say, more lyrical, less afraid of con-
cluding. And rhyme, of course, is to me a
balance not only of sounds, but a balance
which implies agreement. That's why, I suppose, I'd stayed away from rhymes in the early
poems except for this kind of ironic throwback
on what was being said.

Ossman: You have engaged in a considerable
correspondence with other poets on the subject
of poetic techniques. Do you think that this
"talking through letters" has made you an influence upon many of them?

Creeley: It's been an influence on me. Pound
once said that whenever a group of people begin
to communicate with one another, something happens. I've learned tremendously from the correspondence with Paul Blackburn, with Denise
Levertov, with Charles Olson with whom I had
this contact for five years prior to meeting
him. As I've said somewhere, Olson was a practical college of information and stimulus for
me. I suppose, equally, I've had some contact
or influence with others in that same sense. I
believe in handing everything over. If I find
anything of use, I try to get it as quickly as
possible to whomever I consider might use it.

Pass it on. Recently, at a college reading
again, a student said to me, and I can understand what was meant, "When you hear something
you really want to say, don't you in that sense,
not want to say it? Because if you say it, then
it's gone and you don't have it anymore." Well,
in any of these issues I've lived or believed
that by such communication I find a life, and
perhaps it will be, in no specious sense, of
use to others. So if I've had influence, I
hope it's been of that kind. In other words,
just now, I'm not as yet clear on what's being done with "deep image." But they need a
base for writing, and that seems to be theirs
for now. Perhaps they will show more than I
intend to recognize at the moment.

Ossman: What do you understand by "deep image?"

Creeley: It's the question of symbol. I don't
want to say "picture" because that's not accu-
rate. It's what is in the poem as a kind of
statement in the sense "a house," "a car," "a
field"--the image projected by the statement
--as opposed to how the statement is registered.
I can't really discuss with any responsibility
what they are involved with. They seem to come
primarily from the French Symbolists--or specifically I think the Surrealists, the German
Expressionist writers of the period just around
the First World War--Trakl, Gottfried Benn, and
now the present German writers who seem to have
reasserted that interest. The Spanish writers
such as Lorca, Jimenez and Machado, people of
this order whose poems are a fabric of images.
There's no other adequate word for it, I'm
afraid. Lorca was writing, as I understand it,
in a very traditionally settled form--either
folk ballads or else other forms more developed
in the Spanish tradition--so his issue as he
wrote was not to change these forms as, say, an
American poet might now take on that job in
his own tradition, but to learn how to use
them to carry a content important to himself

and finally and even consequently to others.
Lorca's primary quality seems the lucidity in
his line and this curiously moving image or
images which he can carry in his poems. That
is what I believe the "deep imagists" are beginning with. They're going much deeper than
that--"deep image" is "deep"--ok.

Ossman: Everytime I see "1945-1960" on the
cover of the Allen anthology, I get a slightly
apocalyptic feeling . . .

Creeley: Like a tombstone . . .

Ossman: Yes. And I have the feeling that 1960
was a year of reconsideration and evaluation,
despite all the normal activity . . .

Creeley: Again, let me use the occasion of
these students I've been talking with. Ten
years ago everyone was much interested in anthropology and the humanistic sciences. Interested in the question of origins, of how the
concept of culture could be extended in that
sense. Just now the parallel people, the
students now in college, seem very concerned
with theories of knowledge, with communications
systems--with the autonomic nervous system,
for example. With what people like Skinner
and Joshua Whatmough are doing with the statis-
tical analysis of languages and all the problems
of control. That's where William Burroughs
becomes interesting. *Naked Lunch* is about control, however much it's about other things too.
I see what you mean by a sense of conclusion.
I don't think it is *a* conclusion. It's one
conclusion--men arrive at many conclusions in
their lives, in all senses. I think that in
1945, remembering that that's an arbitrary
date, a war had ended, and men of my particular
generation felt almost an immediate impatience
with what was then to be regarded as a solution.
Many of us had been involved in this huge glo-
bal nightmare, and we came back to our specific

personal lives, situations, feeling a great
confusion and at times a great resentment about
what had been given us as a rationale for all
this. So we had that reason to move upon some-
thing--upon a clarity that could confront these
dilemmas more adequately than the generalities
we had been given.

We also had, of course, the very specific
example of William Carlos Williams, who, in
1945, I don't think was even regarded as a
minor poet. It's curious to remember that.
Somewhere around 1950-55 I remember reading
an article in the *Hudson Review* in which he
was dismissed as a "paranoid mumbler." Now
the same journal today would not make the same
statement. So there's been that change.

I feel almost as though we will not have to
go back, but of course we'll now have to qualify ourselves again. The revolution, or at
least the "minor renaissance" that Kenneth Rexroth mentioned in the *New York Times*, is this
period. I feel I'm just getting started, in
other words. I'm not saying this like Sam
Smiles, but everytime I look at what I've done,
I wonder. I've done it, so now I have something else to do. I can't rest, in that sense.
There's no rest for the wicked--again, a New
Englandism.

Ossman: You've mentioned New England several
times. You were born in Massachusetts, weren't
you?

Creeley: Yes, in Arlington, just outside of
Boston. But I actually grew up in a pretty
rural background--on a farm, although it wasn't
actually worked as one. It gave me that kind
of atmosphere, and gave me that sense of speech
as a laconic, ironic, compressed way of saying
something to someone. To say as little as possible as often as possible.

Ossman: You were involved with the beginning
of Cid Corman's magazine *Origin*, were you not?

Creeley: Yes. In fairness to Cid I ought to make very clear that it was his editing and his work that made *Origin* what it subsequently proved. What had happened was simply that I had got in contact with Cid through the radio program he then had, and we weren't satisfied with what we found in available poets. I guess the men we might have looked to were pretty much tied up in other senses. Remember the poetry that comes out of the thirties and forties is a socially orientated poetry. By that I mean that it is engaged primarily with problems of sociology--either ironic comment upon urbane or urban situations, or else a continuing of a tradition of that kind, say, from Ransom, Tate and such older men. William Jay Smith is an instance, Randall Jarrell partly an instance, and Karl Shapiro very much an instance of this kind of writing. We wanted to bring our terms of writing up to the actual poem we were writing. We didn't want to remember anything. We wanted to have the actual issue of the poem in the poem as we were writing it. So Cid got in touch with Olson and Denise Levertov and Paul Blackburn, and that began it, I think.

Ossman: What about the Divers Press, which printed many first volumes of poetry?

Creeley: Well, I think many writers begin by taking on the problem of getting their work printed. I wanted a press that would be of use to specific people, including myself. I printed two of my own books, two of Blackburn's, and I printed Olson, Irving Layton and so on. We had to. We had to have the dignity of our own statement. We had to have it in a form that could be available to other people. So, we were lucky enough to be in a place where there was inexpensive printing to be got, and we were off. I think Jonathan Williams has done a great deal in this same area. I think of recent correspondence with James Purdy. He

printed his first books himself, and luckily
Edith Sitwell saw a copy. In other words, you
cannot get your poems out where they ought to
be if you don't do something about it. So we
put our books out. God, we were laughed at,
but that was part of it too.

[David Ossman: *The Sullen Art*.
New York: Corinth Books, 1963]

ROBERT CREELEY IN
CONVERSATION WITH
CHARLES TOMLINSON

Tomlinson came to Creeley's home in Placitas,
New Mexico, for this interview in the late
spring of 1963.

Tomlinson: I suppose what we are going to say
can find its due occasion in the fact of Donald
Hall's anthology, *Contemporary American Poetry*,
of last year, with its attempt to register for
the English reader the Williamsite bias of much
recent American poetry, and also in the fact
that we are finally on the eve of the publica-
tion of William Carlos Williams in England.
We'll doubtless have cause to come back to Williams, but I would like to begin with you, Robert. I was reading recently a review by Donald
Davie in which he spoke of your poetry and
Charles Olson's prose as showing the modern
movement in art taking on "a new lease of unexpected life." An Englishman, of course, is un-
willing to admit that Olson writes poetry as
well as prose. However, the main implication
behind what Davie was saying seems to be a feeling that somehow the modern movement, ushered
in by Eliot and Pound and Schoenberg and Webern
and the cubists, or whatever, has somehow broken
down. Now do you, as an American writer, feel
this break in the continuity of modern art,
specifically poetry?

Creeley: No, not very, actually. I think that
what's happened, at least in the context of the

States, is that the poetry of the Twenties and
Thirties, or that which was dominant at that time,
publicly--let's say the poetry of Ransom and
Tate and Bishop and that which then came from
the younger men such as Jarrell--this poetry,
in effect, tended to block off, not to smother
but to cover, the actual tradition that was
still operating in the poetry of say Zukofsky
and Reznikoff and George Oppen, but I feel that
the continuity is there, suffers no break, keeps
going. I suppose for one thing the particular
lives of the men involved made it impossible
to have an apparently clear line all the time.
Of those concerned, there's the fact that Pound
was living abroad, H.D. was in Europe also, and
Williams was living a life which defined him
primarily as a doctor. Zukofsky is very quiet
and not at all a man who enjoys asserting himself publicly. So I think that what happened
was that once the social aspect of the Roaring
Twenties died out in writing, people assumed
that the actual work that had been initiated
in that same period was done too, but we find
that people actually worked continuously all
during the time: besides Williams and Zukofsky
there is H.D., and the younger men who were dis-
satisfied with the Ransom and Tate school went
to them. They were happily available in some
sense.

Tomlinson: Would you say that Pound, then, was
the primary source in this continuity that your
generation feels?

Creeley: I think so. I think that his great virtue, at least for younger men in this country,
was, first of all, that he gave us a sense of
how to be responsible in relation to writing
either as a writer or equally as a reader. He
gave a very succinct and clear and utterly un-
mistakable body of attitudes for reading poetry.
I don't think any other critic has given something so immediately useful.

Tomlinson: In this, Pound provided a sound in-
oculation for you against the New Critics?

Creeley: Yes. In other words, he warned against
the muzziness that can come of a too conscious
fuddling of symbolism. I remember recently (I
think it's Bridson), in a radio interview with
Pound, makes reference to a set of frescoes in
Italy, and Pound's comment is, "No, no, that's
symbolism. I wasn't interested in that." In
other words, although to Bridson it seemed that
this would be parallel, Pound has always been
intent to make a very clear demarcation between
a symbol which in effect exhausts its references
as opposed to a sign or mark of something which
constantly renews its reference.

Tomlinson: What you say of Pound would seem to
link very much with your own poetry. I recall
that when the *Times Literary Supplement* once
mentioned your poem, "I Know a Man," where the
name John occurs and someone says, "for Christ's
sake," in the *T.L.S.* account, both John and
Christ had to be gone into deeply on a very
symbolic level. I think this is the kind of
thing the English tend to do when they read
Williams, when they read Pound, when they read
you: they can't take what you're presenting--
they must somehow try to dig down for something
which they think ought to be there and they get
frustrated when they find it isn't.

Creeley: Well, again, I suppose that's partly
due to the fact that the two cultures are separated really by the terms of a whole spiritual
environment. I mean, when one lives in the
States, even so recently as, say, my own childhood, the terms of that environment are most
usually ones that demand an immediate recognition of facts and substantial data in that environment. Now this is what Williams meant, I
think, when he said, "No ideas but in things."
It's the old characteristic that has become so
associated with American pragmatism.

Tomlinson: This, then, is where Williams comes back into our picture in that he interprets the terms of environment as given by New Jersey. Do you think this makes him too much of a local poet? The English attitude seems very much to be that Williams is strictly not for export.

Creeley: Well, I know, for example, of your own interest in Machado, and I certainly think of Chaucer and a number of other major figures of all nationalities who depended on, let's say, a very particular, close local reference for the substance of their detail. This has been remarked over and over and I don't think Williams' emphasis upon a body of local detail has limited him any more than it has Chaucer or Machado . . . I'm sentimental enough to believe that one proceeds from the immediate and particular--this is where the universal is to be embodied, if anywhere.

Tomlinson: I always feel myself that one ought to be able to take up with Williams at the level of discourse. Hugh Kenner has a marvelous description of this where he says that Williams in his verse presents "the continuous fascination of watching word succeed word like the sections of a telescope opening, as though nothing more mysterious were at work than natural discourse; and simultaneously of observing the whole sequence of words arch through space and vanish with a single echo in a way no natural discourse could manage." I'm sure that if once one taps Williams on that level, one can really take the localism.

Creeley: I think (very much with reference to Kenner's point) that Williams himself has given us a succinct definition of his own intent: when he says, for example, that a poet *thinks* with his poem and this itself is the profundity. In other words, a poem can be an instance of all the complexity of a way of thinking. Williams makes us aware of all the emotional conflicts involved in the act of thinking, so that you get apparent juxtapositions of feeling in a Williams poem that would not be understandable unless one were to take it literally as the context in which the mind has shifted to another point of contact in the very writing. There is no unity of view, let's say, in the more classical sense. It's not something that Williams, I think, even considered interesting. I mean, not to him as a man. He knew that you change your mind every time you see something, and--what is it he says?--"A new world is only a new mind." So the context is continually what you can feel and where you are.

Tomlinson: Now you mentioned Zukofsky, who has remained even more unknown in England than Williams himself. At least, one sees Williams in anthologies, whereas, apart from Pound's *Active Anthology*, of long, long ago, and Ian Finlay's recent printing of *Sixteen Once Published*, Zukofsky has had no innings at all. What do you feel Zukofsky has to teach the contemporary writer that Williams hasn't?

Creeley: Well, suppose we go back to the sense of continuity we began with. It's interesting that in the printing of Zukofsky's long poem, *A* (and I think it's actually longer than the twelve books included in this printing), it's gone on, it's a continuous poem much akin in nature of purpose to Pound's *Cantos*. The poem's composition extends from the twenties to the fifties, at least. It's a day book, or journal, and attempts to deal with reality over a man's life. Zukofsky feels that one writes the same poem all one's life and that it is purposeless to try to say, "Gee, you know, I wrote a great poem in 56 and now I've written a bad poem in 1963." There isn't this distinction to be made in a man's work.

Tomlinson: But would you say this is very different from Williams in *Paterson*?

Creeley: Yes. I have always experienced a kind
of equivocal reaction on my own part to that
particular work. Sections of that poem are fabu-
lous, but Charles Olson's qualifying comment
I've always felt is relevant to its prominence;
the one in *Mayan Letters* where Olson says that
Williams doesn't seem to have known what the
whole complex of a city was. Now Williams grew
up when Rutherford was a small town. He saw the
town change in his occupation as a doctor. But
I don't think that he was either interested or
equipped, in a sense, to deal with the recognition of the city that Rutherford became, and
certainly Paterson is even more complicated--
an instance of an industrial, ugly city, but
nonetheless a very substantial one. Well, Williams' reaction to Zukofsky was always that he
felt he couldn't understand a word he was saying. In short, what Zukofsky has done is to
take distinctions of both ear and intelligence
to a fineness that is difficult. It is difficult to follow a man when he's thinking very
closely. And it's extremely difficult to follow him when he's using all the resources that
he has developed or inherited regarding the
particular nature of words as sound. I think
Zukofsky is a very conscious artist; I can't
think of another man in the States, with the
possible exception of Robert Duncan and Olson,
perhaps, who approaches the consciousness with
which he writes. If you read his translations
of Catullus in which he is trying, in effect,
to transpose or transliterate, or whatever the
word would be, the texture of Latin sound into
American language, it's an extraordinary *tour
de force*. No, I find that in this whole thing
that Pound came into--the tone leading of vowels,
the question of measure, the question of the
total effect in terms of sound and sight of a
given piece of poetry--these aspects are tremendously handled by Zukofsky as by no one else.

Tomlinson: I have the impression that to get

anything like the musical cohesiveness of the
best of Zukofsky's lyrics, you simply have got
to go back to the Elizabethans, to someone like
Campion. Having spoken of Pound, Williams and
Zukofsky, there's another figure I would like
to ask you about--do you feel that anything is
left from Cummings today?

Creeley: No, because Cummings' battle with the
typographical set of the poem was one in which,
once people were willing to admit typography
could be variable and could have a useful effect,
the particular value was lost--like suffrage,
once women were given the vote. (I have a difficult time feeling much involvement with people
who fought for suffrage because, I mean, now
we have it, so to speak.)

Tomlinson: With Cummings, presumably, the poem
goes on losing its energies in a kind of jittery
futurism?

Creeley: I feel so. I like some of his earlier
poems very much, both the uses of the sonnet
and some of the straight wise-guy poems where
you get this beautiful jargon and slang, but I
feel that he's always been limited by being a
real college boy, by which I mean that his thinking, curiously, has never really gone deeper
than the kind of, oh! let's say junior, sophomore, college wit.

Tomlinson: Also, when he wants to convince one,
he can get dangerously vibrato. But do you feel
that what you've said so far is quite fair to
the kind of thing that Cummings has done in
prose--in *Eimi*, for example?

Creeley: Well, could I make one footnote on
Cummings? Perhaps one can't do him quite so
simply as I seem to have done. I certainly feel
that his prose is very interesting. *The Enormous
Room* is a classic of its kind, and *Eimi*, I agree,
is a real book. And I was interested, too, in

Pound's sense of Cummings as being equivalent, in Pound's estimation, to a writer like Catullus. Now, I've never, frankly, felt that the two men ever were--this is Pound's curiously ambivalent sense of love. That's the only thing that I ever feel is a generality in Pound: the intensity or substance of love.

Tomlinson: What the age needs is a Catullus, so Pound, out of love, undertakes to supply one?

Creeley: Yes, it certainly does, but I don't think it was Cummings.

Tomlinson: Now the reason I brought up Cummings was that I have seen people write about his presence in your own work. I've always found this rather difficult to sound. I take it that your work has been given much more its direction by a poet like Charles Olson?

Creeley: Well, I think one could dispose quite easily of the question of my poems' being like Cummings by reference to the sense of an audience. I don't have an audience, and this qualifies what I write. My poems are limited, unhappily perhaps, by having to speak in a very single fashion. I don't speak for a generality of people. Now Cummings, despite all his insistence on the single identity of the "i," is speaking for almost a class.

Tomlinson: Do you feel that Olson's manifesto, "Projective Verse," has altered very appreciably the direction in which you yourself are moving?

Creeley: Well, it did. But things began back in 1949, when a friend and I were trying to start a magazine and looking for a nucleus of contributors. When I got some poems of Olson's, I remember writing back, in a sort of glib fashion one has at twenty-two or twenty-three or whatever age I was, that this man was simply looking for a language, and, WOW, I got a beautiful

letter from Olson saying, "What do you mean?"
Not just mad, but just saying, "Come on, let's
talk about this," and that started the correspondence. Well, he was tremendously articulate
and clear apropos my own work and he started
to show me where habits and attitudes toward
the line were really not only blocking the particular emotional intensity that I was working
for, but he showed me how the whole way of
speech was not true to the way I was thinking.
And then those letters actually became incor-
porated finally in that essay on projective
verse--in the first section, where he is talking about the significance of the syllable,
the sense of breathing, the sense of where the
intelligence is operating and the choice of
the language where the whole physiology of man
is at work in the poem.

Tomlinson: I think that here's something an
English reader would like to know about: when
Olson says, "the two halves [in poetry] are the
HEAD by way of the EAR to the SYLLABLE, the
HEART by way of the BREATH to the LINE," how
literally are we to understand him? The words
are, surely, primarily metaphoric?

Creeley: Exactly. Take the heart first. One
would misunderstand Olson completely if the
assumption were that he wanted one to take
something like a stopwatch or set a metronome
to the heartbeat.

Tomlinson: I've certainly seen that attitude
taken by reviewers in the American quarterlies.

Creeley: It's absurd. What he is trying to say
is that the heart is a basic instance not only
of rhythm, but it is the base of the measure of
rhythms for all men in the way heartbeat is like
the metronome in their whole system. So that
when he says the heart by way of the breath to
the line, he is trying to say that it is in the
line that the basic rhythmic scoring takes place.

The line, that is, is that unit in a poem
which defines, by the context it creates, the
rhythmic complex of the poem's continuity. You
see, you can't use a single word, you know it
takes words in complex, or words in context to
establish a rhythmic continuity. The line is
that unit which is most basic to the establish-
ing of this rhythmic continuity. This is saying nothing, after all, more difficult than
when one speaks of an iambic pentameter line,
a five-feet line, having this or that character. He is saying that what we have to know
how to do is to come to a closer feeling of
what, after all, is the stress complex in a
given unit. And the heart also has to do with
the senses of emotion. When one is excited the
heart beats fast; this, in effect, creates a
quicker rhythm and the breath comes short. Now,
the head, the intelligence by way of the ear
to the syllable--which he calls also "the king
and pin"--is the unit upon which all builds.
The heart, then, stands, as the primary feeling
term. The head, in contrast, is discriminating.
It is discriminating by way of what it hears.
People talk about what they see in a poem--
that's fine--I understand that. A lot of poetry
in our particular period has been written as a
visual occasion, but the finer occasion seems
to be one in which one is *hearing* a poem. I
don't go necessarily with all the hullabaloo
that surrounds public readings, but I think of
all the poetry that's been lost because it wasn't
heard.

Tomlinson: I take it we're really back now to
what Williams was doing. Olson's work, perhaps,
is a continuation of what was implicit in Williams' sense of the line, in his *insistence* on
the line?

Creeley: Yes. Except that I remember asking
Olson what his own feelings were about Williams.
They were quite different men. I think Olson
always did respect Williams and his work, but

Olson wanted something that could encompass a
whole cultural reality, whereas Williams, I
don't think, until the late instance of *Paterson*, was really interested in this. He was much
more interested in what we perhaps could simply
call a projected impression, but defined with
all possible intelligence of that perception.
Olson, however, wanted something that could
encompass and deal with all the variability of
presence in a total social organism. Now, in
that sense, he's much more akin to Pound. I
think Olson found Pound to be the most definitive of the poets prior to himself, at least
in the American scene. But Olson has always
been irritated by the fact that Pound's back
wall is, let's say, fifth century B.C. He goes
right there and stops. Olson himself wants to
push it back at least to the Hittites and the
Sumerians, wants to think of organizations of
intelligence as pre-Socratic. Also his sense of
economics is very distinct from Pound's. His
sense of the social complex is very distinct.
His background curiously includes, for example,
having been chairman for foreign language groups
for the Democratic Party--I believe it was during
the second time Roosevelt ran for President. So
he was concerned with correcting what he felt to
be errors of Pound's attitude. He wanted to see
the organization of the poem become something more
than an ego system. That again is a qualification
he makes of Pound.

Tomlinson: Well, it would seem, then, that there
has been a very direct continuity and a very
direct conversation carried on in American poetry
ever since the--what?--the twenties?

Creeley: Yes. And those concerned in that conversation, as distinct from the Ransom-Tate nexus,
give you a particular sense of how to deal with
your contemporary reality. Pound does constantly.
Williams does. Olson does, to my sense. Zukofsky
does. And I would rather have to do with men who
are trying to think in terms of contemporary

realities, instead of being awfully-old-Southern-gentleman--I enjoy antiques but I don't want to *make* antiques. I hate fakes, in other words.

Tomlinson: What sort of an organization was Black Mountain College?

Creeley: It began as a protest on the part of a nucleus of teachers at Rollins College, Florida, which was itself an experimental college and started, I think, in the twenties.

Tomlinson: The intellectual force behind Black Mountain would be Dewey, then?

Creeley: Yes, the influence was John Dewey. These people who separated felt they wanted to reorganize their whole conception of teaching, and first of all rented a hotel, a sort of large summer hotel, in Black Mountain, which is a very beautiful North Carolina town. It's curious, though, that they would choose such a place for a college of this kind, because it's also in the heart of the Baptist belt--Billy Graham comes from Black Mountain. So they chose a very reactionary part of the States. Anyhow, the first group was this Deweyism, working to understand the community, with everybody participating. Then, towards the end of the thirties, the next influx of teaching people is the group from the Bauhaus (though Josef Albers was there at the beginning), men of this order, who are thinking of the functional concept of the arts and of the organization of the intelligence generally, but who are not so persuaded by the social ethic. This is the dominant spirit of the college into the forties, with Josef Albers as director. It's in the late forties that Albers leaves and becomes head of the Yale School of Design and, for a time, there was no actual director of the college. Olson became Rector, I think about 51 or 52, and he is head of the college for its last period. First of all it was a college that was directed completely by the teaching body.

There was no board of administrators, no board
of regents, no ownership by an outside agency.
The college was owned and operated by the teach-
ers--each teacher had that situation as soon as
he joined the staff: he was a responsible member
of the whole set-up. At the time I was there the
college had shrunk bitterly: actually the enroll-
ment was way down to about twenty students. I
remember the pay was very small and so all depended on a particular sense of the use of the
place for anyone to come at all.

Tomlinson: You mentioned Albers. I was wondering whether, in your time at Black Mountain,
there was much contact between the writers there
and the painters like Kline and de Kooning.

Creeley: There was. Very substantially. Not with
Albers, but with the people who came in the fifties, primarily for summer teaching--Kline,
Motherwell, de Kooning, Vicente, Guston, and
so on, the painters that became the so-called
action painters, the abstract expressionists.
All of them at that time were, with the possible exception of de Kooning and Kline, just beginning to get some kind of recognition. That
was a very volatile time in their own lives.
The fifties, early fifties, for these painters
is an extraordinary period. There was, yes, a
close rapport.

Tomlinson: Did their mode of operation have anything to do with the way poems were beginning
to be written at that time?

Creeley: Not actually as an example, perhaps,
but it was a reassuring parallel. I think of a
comment by Pollock when he makes a point about
his own work. He says, "When I am in my painting, I am not aware of what I am doing. It is
only after a sort of 'get-acquainted' period
that I see what I have been about. I have no
fears about making changes or destroying images,
because the painting has a life of its own. I

try to let it come through. It is only when I
lose contact that the result is a mess. Otherwise, there is pure harmony and it is easy going."

Tomlinson: You feel that this is a possible way
to talk about the poetic process?

Creeley: Well, this is what Olson, perhaps, is
saying in a parallel manner when he speaks of
the open form or composition by field in "Projective Verse," where you are trying to maintain your relation to the poem you are writing
rather than to some poem somebody else has written. Valéry, in that collection of his essays,
The Art of Poetry, makes a comment on, or definition of, lyric poetry, where the form and
content, he says, are inextricable and where
the form is being discovered at each instant,
where there can be no prior determination of
the form except that which is recognized as the
writing occurs. Now this is parallel to that
sense of Olson's and obviously parallel to Pollock where what you are thinking about is constantly to try to articulate that responsibility
which what you see demands. It's an awfully pre-
carious situation to be in, because you can ob-
literate everything in one instant. You've got
to be utterly awake to recognize what is happening, and to be responsible for all the things
you must do before you can even recognize what
their full significance is. It's like going into
a spin in a car--you use all the technical information you have about how to get that car
back on the road, but you're not thinking "I
must bring the car back on the road," you are
bringing the car back on the road or else you're
over the cliff.

Tomlinson: All this would seem to be part of
Olson's insistence that you move rapidly from
one perception to another in a poem or simply
bog down.

Creeley: Yes. He says that one thing must immediately follow another and what he is getting at is the too-frequent habit among certain writers where the man is just talking round and round, without having taken his particular insight to any terms of possibility, without transmission of energy.

Tomlinson: At the back of what you are saying and what Olson is saying, I seem to catch a sharp echo of Fenollosa's essay on the Chinese written character as a medium for poetry, as edited by Pound, with its stress on the verb as the transmitter of energy.

Creeley: Yes, that is a really important document for the whole development of American poetry since Pound.

Tomlinson: And how would you evaluate this concept, "energy," as it keeps appearing in any discussion of American art?

Creeley: Well, one could use Robert Duncan's too little known essay on Olson's work. In Olson's aesthetic--and Duncan sees this as having "forelightings," as he calls it, in Emerson and Dewey --in Olson's aesthetic, "conception cannot be abstracted from doing, beauty is related to the beauty of an archer hitting the mark"--he's thinking again of Pound. And then he goes on to contrast the *visual* spirit of Italian fourteenth-century with the *muscular* spirit of American twentieth-century painting. Furthermore, he underlines the difference between energy referred to (*seen*), as in the Vorticists and the Futurists, and energy embodied in the painting (*felt*) which is now "muscular as well as visual," as he says, "contained as well as apparent." And he instances Hofmann, Pollock and Kline. Now that aspect, you see, is common to all the arts in America. It's equally common to the present experiments of John Cage, where the whole attention is literally centered on what an act is.

Tomlinson: Your speaking of Robert Duncan brings to mind--despite some broad agreements of theory --just how different from one another are the whole company of poets associated with Black Mountain and who appeared in the *Black Mountain Review* with you as editor. I am thinking of the kind of variety as between yourself and Duncan, and again as between Duncan and Denise Levertov, or Paul Blackburn and Gary Snyder. In editing *Black Mountain Review*, were you looking for poetry with any special kind of a common factor, so to speak?

Creeley: Well, not altogether. I had, by that time, like it or not, a sense of what poetry I respected, but I was willing to print pieces that certainly went beyond any kind of poetry that I personally wrote. In the *Black Mountain Review* the content and manner of the poetry ranged quite wide in terms of the writing: there are some poems there by Duncan which are very curious--a period in which he was inter- ested in learning from Gertrude Stein.

Tomlinson: One last question. Of all the great of the older generation, we have not mentioned Eliot. Do you think that Eliot is still avail- able to the American poet as a useful influence?

Creeley: No. Eliot is far less available than the people we have spoken of. And there is one much earlier poet who is far, far more available than Eliot . . .

Tomlinson: And that is?

Creeley: That is the figure the New Critics and the universities to this day have conspired to ignore: that is Walt Whitman.

[*The Review* 10, January 1964]

CONTEXTS OF POETRY:
WITH ALLEN GINSBERG
IN VANCOUVER

Fred Wah taped the body of the text at the University of British Columbia Poetry Conference, the morning of 24 July 1963; and it was transcribed by George F. Butterick.

Creeley: What Allen suggested, and what I thought would be a good idea, would be to begin with some sense of writing in the most literal of possible contexts. Now the supposition, I suppose, on the part of some of you who've come, is that we write poetry; in other words, this is what we do. And we, in effect, have been given a definition publicly as poets. We've published books and all the rest. But that kind of qualification is something I'd not like to take on, in this or any other context. So I would like to take up the issue of writing as a physical act. What I will tell you is how I write, and Allen, then you take it from there, you do the same. In other words, I want to speak of what is involved in writing for me.
   When I first met William Carlos Williams, for instance, I remember he took me upstairs to show me where the bathroom was, and as we went by the--I think the bedroom--he showed me the desk that had been in his office when he was in active practice; and he showed me his typewriter, which was a large old office machine, and the way it fitted under the desk;

and he showed me the prescription pads that
he used to use. And again, Allen and I were
thinking of how the qualification of the size
of the paper, for example, will often have an
effect on what you're writing, or whether or
not you're using a pencil or a pen. Habits
of this kind are almost always considered immaterial or secondary. And yet, for my own
reality, there is obviously a great connection between what I physically do as a writer
in this sense, and what comes then out of it.
So I want briefly to qualify it. I was curious to know how I do it myself, in the sense
of what really do I do. Well, say, first of
all, I write always with a typewriter. I get
very nervous about using a pen, because pens
run out of ink in a way . . . ball points are
what I would use, as and when I do write that
way . . . pencils have to be sharpened, I get
so involved with the sharpening of the pencil.
Also, I think it goes back to a sense I had
when younger, that typewriters, typewriting,
implied a "professional" context. If you were
going to be serious, or going to *claim* seriousness for yourself, the instrument that you
used in writing had to be particular to what
the act of writing was. So that I had, I
think, a basically naive sense of this kind.
I wanted to be able to do it with a typewriter.
Now, equally, I never learned to type. So I
mean my typing is a habit that's developed,
with two fingers. I never took a class in
high school or any other place that taught me
how to use the full, you know, all your fingers when you're typing. Think again--that
begins to be a qualification of how *fast* I
can write. In other words, I find that the
pace of my writing is concerned with the speed
with which I can type. Now, I can type actually about as fast as I can talk, with two fingers. I find, for example, if I have to work
on somebody else's typewriter, I'm displaced,
because there may be a slight variation in the
space between keys. I find that now I can use

the typewriter I do use without looking at it,
so that I can be thinking of something without consciously wondering where my fingers
are. I find . . . let's see, I want to keep
on a little bit in this sense of what the
physical conditions are . . . because again,
I started writing in a context where I was
embarrassed. I didn't want to bother anybody.
I didn't want, you know, like, don't mind me,
but just go right ahead with what you're doing, with your *serious business*, with your
serious preoccupation. This was primarily in
a former marriage, and the problems thereof
. . . I didn't want to call attention to myself, because doing that might force me to
define what I was trying to do--which is obviously impossible. So, the next thing I
would do would be to create a context in which
there was a residuum of noise, constantly
present, so that my own noise wouldn't be intrusive. And so I find often I turn on the
radio. I used to--back in New Hampshire,
where I think I really sat down to think of
how to write or what to write--I used to play
records all the time. We had at that time, I
remember, one of these big Jensen speakers
and all, and amplifier, and I'd put on the
records that I then much valued, as Charlie
Parker and what not--but just because that
rhythmic insistence, I think, kept pushing me,
I kept hearing it. And lately, for example,
in the last year, I finished a long prose
work, a novel, and I found that what I was
writing could be actually stimulated by playing particular kinds of music. In other words,
I don't know . . . I'm not a psychologist or
even interested in this aspect, what I'm . . .

Ginsberg: What kind of music?

Creeley: Well, for example, the whole first
part of *The Island* is written primarily to an
old Bud Powell tape, a record, where you get
these great kinds of almost concert style . . .

let's say a poor man's concept of beauty, you
know, where you get these great crescendos of
sound, and where you get actually a basically
simple melody, as "I Got Rhythm" or anything,
playing through this, and then you get this
involvement that constantly comes back to the
simple statement because it's embarrassed
actually with its own hope. So this first
part of the novel is written in that sense.
Then the whole middle section is written primarily to John Coltrane, where you get deli-
berate dissonance and you get fragmentation
--I wasn't conscious of this--and then the
last part is written to a kind of Nancy Wil-
son, you know, where you get a "where love is
gone," dig? And you get a *real slick* preten-
sion. In other words, where she's singing,
in effect, the memory of some authenticity
which she no longer even . . . she never meant
it. I saw her on television and . . . she's
no slicker than any professional, but she's
singing in a manner which is now a *manner*.
She's not an innovator, as was Sarah Vaughan,
or, more particularly, Billie Holiday. Again,
the middle section involves Billie Holiday.
But what I'm trying to say is: so, that's a
physical requirement for me. I find it very
useful for me . . .

Ginsberg: Even in poems?

Creeley: Even in poems. It also gives me
something to do when I'm not doing anything.
It gives me something to focus on or to relax
back into as a place where I feel safe. Anyhow: the typewriter, the insistence of music,
rhythm, something with a strong rhythmic character, not *too* loud, subtle enough so that you
can always go back to it . . . and paper. Usually an 8" by 11" sheet. I best like, most
like, the yellow copy paper that's not spongy,
but has a softness to it, so that when you
type, the letter goes in, embeds a little. I
hate a hard paper. When you erase this paper

you take a layer off. And I remember again
--now this is why I want to point out, this
is not ridiculous--because I remember one
time when living in Spain, there was none
of this particular size copy paper that I
was used to using. So I got a legal size
sheet. And it was suddenly a terror, because I would finish what was normally my
habit of dealing with the paper and realize
that I had about six inches left at the bot-
tom that was blank. This set up a whole different feeling. I remember writing a story
actually using this paper, and it seemed to
me that things were taking an awfully long
time. In other words, the whole balance
or pattern of the way of working with the
thing was being changed. So the paper is
significant. Again, Allen and I were talking about the way Jack Kerouac . . . the
qualification of his writing that occurs
when he is working in small notebooks. Or
I could say the same of Robert Duncan, for
example, who uses a notebook and writes in
ink, and the composition of his books is
obviously done as he's writing. There is,
for example, an actual instance of a book
of this kind that he did, called *Fragments
of a Disorderd Devotion*, in which it's re-
produced from the actual . . . well, actually he wrote it as a copy of his own manner. It's an imitation of his manner by
himself, so it has that . . .   But you
realize that it's all happening visually
as well as intellectually or mentally.
Olson, in his letters . . . you begin to
realize Olson's spacing, the ordering of
where things occur in his thought. He'll
begin a letter like, "dear so and so," and
then start with the information, and before
he's, say, halfway through the page you've
got these things jumping all around . . .
the movement, is moving, trying to locate,
like, let's put that there . . . no don't,
now this goes here, oh but you can't forget

that . . . but you can't forget this too . . .
you can't put them like that, because it's a
lie, they don't exist that way, you've got to
. . . He's trying in effect to give the *orders*
of thought--in no pretentious sense--and a
typewriter for him, for example, is something
that has much defined his habits of writing,
as he said himself in "Projective Verse." But
equally, he has a speed in handwriting that's
fast, a very fast style of writing . . .

But positions and textures of paper, en-
velopes and what not . . . I find again that
in order to be taken seriously by myself that
I again had to create a context in which I
could exhibit the instance of professionalism.
I remember some friend, for example, who said
he always washed his hands before he started
to write, because he wanted to be clean, he
didn't want to get anything dirty. I can remember equally, when I had run out of paper
. . . the circumstances of living at some
remote place . . . I would really get . . . it
would be awful. And then you'd start to impro-
vise paper from envelopes--but very carefully
folding them and all but ironing them out to
get the right feeling. What I'm trying to say
with all this rambling, is that the particular
habits of writing that you begin to develop
will have, curiously, a great significance for
what you write. If you think I'm fooling, you
might for example try to see what happens if
you write with different kinds of media. In
other words, try writing with large crayons,
or--I wish we had access to this--it would be
interesting to see what happens if you try to
write on something the size of this blackboard.
I taught first grade also . . . I remember this
. . . where you're writing things like [*moves
to blackboard*] . . . I could do this, in teaching handwriting . . . Now, I can't write like
this, I get so absorbed, involved with the
voluptuousness, the sensuous . . . it's distracting to me. Because what I'm trying to
do, if I'm successful . . . I am not antici-

pating any content before it occurs. At the
same time, I'm trying to recognize, or rather,
I'm awfully bewildered by confusions between
certain terms--the states of consciousness--
e.g. the difference between recognition, understanding, realization, knowing. I'm trying
to describe a state in which one primarily
feels what is happening as a fit balance. If
you do things like ski or swim or drive, for
example, you know that sense of feeling when
the car is operating smoothly, when the balance of the steering and the movement of the
car is coinciding with an intention of your
own and is following with a sense of grace,
an appropriateness. Everything is, in effect,
falling into place. You're not intentionally
putting it there, but you're recognizing the
feeling of its occurring there. So that when
I'm writing myself, if something becomes dis-
sonant or something becomes jarred, arbitrarily, then I have to stop. One other thing I
should note, also about the sense of the physical act of writing, is that the same habit of
wanting it to be "perfect" in its appearance,
means that if I'm writing and I make a mistake, I take the paper out and copy it down
to that point, correct the mistake, and then
throw the paper away. In other words, I have
a great difficulty writing on the paper. For
example, I can never write in books. And I
get awfully upset if other people write in my
book . . . writing in my book . . . seeing
dirty hands all over my book . . . Because
I don't really think that I can own a book. I
don't think that I have the *right*, to write.

In college itself . . . now let's go back
there, because that's where we are again . . .
I was in the context of other younger men of
that time who wanted to be writers also . . .
Donald Hall, for example--that was in Harvard
in 1946, a group which then centered around
Wake--Seymour Lawrence, now editor for Atlantic
Monthly Press, Kenneth Koch. I remember, say,
Kenneth Koch one time invited me up to his rooms

for, I think it was sherry, and to listen to
records, like Bach and what not, and to read
me a few poems. Well, I can remember going
up to his room, and it was, you know, it was
a very comfortable room. Kenneth comes from
a family that has money, and so that was evident in his room. It had very tasteful repro-
ductions, there was furniture that he'd bought
. . . I couldn't do that. At that time I
wasn't writing anything that I felt was that
significant. I mean I was desperate to understand what would actually be a poem. Again,
as Allen and I were talking yesterday--you've
really come at a good time!--because I think
each of us in our own circumstances has come
to that point where the very definition of a
poem as a possibility, not as a possibility
perhaps, but as an actual construct, is something we are very unable to state like that.
In other words, I cannot define a poem. It's
a curious state of mind to have arrived at.
I cannot tell you what I think a poem is. I
think that has to do with the fact that all
the terms of consciousness are, at the moment,
undergoing tremendous terms of change. We
were again talking, thinking of the context
now in the States. There is an alteration of
a very deep order going on in the whole thrust
or push of the consciousness, literally the
Negro consciousness, that has been for years
relegated to a kind of underside or underworld.
As Duncan says, "I see always the underside
turning . . ." Well, see, the Negro personali-
ty in the States has been forced to live in
this underside world, except in contexts which
he could control. LeRoi Jones, for example,
grew up in a fairly secure middle-class background that had, let's say, the securities of
that status. But you see, there was always a
limit to it. You could always take one step
beyond the control of the neighborhood and you
were suddenly in a world which was utterly un-
responsive to your reality. Now this reality,
which has become *the* dominant reality in the

States today, is the Negro reality, it is not
the white reality, it's the Negro reality.
You may want to interpret the activities of
the Kennedys as large, liberal recognitions
that have been long overdue, but I think it
would be utterly naive to do so. I think that
the Kennedys are being washed along in a shift
that is not only located in the States but--
now Allen can tell you much more accurately
these terms--but is coming from a whole shift
of controls and communication terms that are
actually centered in Africa and Asia.
    I don't want to take us too far afield, but
my point is that the very premise on which
consciousness operates is undergoing modifications that none of us, I think, are at the
moment capable of defining. We can only recognize them. Let's say, that if Pound says
artists are the antennae of the race, I think
that any of us here is in a position to be
responsive to this feeling that's so immense,
so definite, and so insistent. Not because
we can *do* anything with it. It simply is, it's
a big change, it's a deep change in consciousness, and I'm curious to see what's going to
happen--which is a mild way of putting it.
Indeed! But you have a poem, Allen, in which
you say, "Where all Manhattan that I've known
must disappear." And this for me is what is
happening in the States in a different relationship, in a different context--where all the
terms of consciousness that I grew up with must
disappear, are disappearing momently, daily.
The terms of reality are changing. Even the
terms of this course are changing . . . by
which I mean, this course would have been impossible ten years ago, by definition. Senses
of writing would have been impossible to present in this fashion ten years ago. We were,
happily, involved with a reorganization of
premise that gave us our particular occasion.
Yours is going to be perhaps even more a mess.
I mean that I think that the change which is
occurring now is more significant than the

Second World War by far, because it's the resi-
due of that war in reference to the atom bomb
and, equally, the shift in *all* terms of human
relationship that have been habitualized since,
oh God, thousands of years. This goes back
to correct, not to correct, but to reorganize
premises that have existed for thousands of
years, concepts of person . . . Look, I'd
like *you* to talk for a while . . .

Ginsberg: The last time I wrote was on a train
from Kyoto to Tokyo. I suddenly had a great
seizure of realization, on a whole bunch of
levels. I was thinking of a poetic problem
which is not along lines . . . It's another
matter. Also, about an emotional problem which
was just resolving itself. And I was suddenly
having feelings for the first time, certain
kinds of feelings for the first time in about
a half year. I was feeling something that had
been growing and growing and growing and all of
a sudden appeared to me on the train. So I
had to get it then because I knew in an hour
when I got to Tokyo I'd be all hung up in Tokyo
--you know, looking for a room in Tokyo--and
I'd be having other feelings, or going back to
material problems of arranging things. But
here I had that moment and . . . That's what
I don't understand about your writing, what
happens to you if you suddenly realize some-
thing--do you have to--arrange your paper?
What do you do then--you lose it!

Creeley: You're right! No, I was just thinking as you were saying this, that the limit of
my ability to write, at the moment, and has
been for the last two years, is that I have to
secure a physical context in which I can "work."
It not only has to be qualified by having
paper and the rest of the paraphernalia, but
it has to have equally a social qualification.
I remember, for example, friends walking in
when I'm working. I literally stop. I cannot
work when someone's looking at me. So that, I

envy you. I remember . . . again this experience of knowing both you and Jack [Kerouac] in
San Francisco, and Jack equally will walk always with a notebook and be writing away. Or
Robert Duncan, again . . . That's why I suppose I always end up living in these circumstances that are very isolate, in other words,
where I won't be disturbed. Yet I don't think
it's a pretentious thing. It's frankly a need
I . . .

Ginsberg: What you set up . . . does that actually catalyze feelings?

Creeley: It seems to create a context in which
those feelings can occur. The thing is that
I'm so shy--in no specious or stupid sense--but
I'm so worried about keeping myself together
when I'm in public, so to speak, as even now.
I mean these habits of speaking are, after all,
the habits that I got from teaching. But when
I'm writing, you see, that business of Olson's,
"He left him naked,/ the man said, and/ naked-
ness/ is what one means . . ." In order to be
in that state of nakedness, I have to be where
--it isn't so much distraction--but where I
can open up this equally small thing, and feel
it with the intensity of all the perception
that I . . . that the ego bit can recognize,
and then destroy the ego by its own insistence.
It's shy in other words . . .

Ginsberg: Situated where there is no threat . . .

Creeley: Well, equally, it's an . . . see, I
would be embarrassed for years. I remember
when I got to the Southwest, the people there
have a very easy and pleasant habit of embrac-
ing one another when they meet; that is, in-laws
or friends. It took me *years*! I was, frankly,
when I saw you for example, I was so pleased
that I could put my arms around you as an old
friend and hold on to you. It took me years
to be able to do that, and maybe one day I'll

be able to do this too. I'm not satisfied with
the habits of limit that I've created for myself, because not only have I given myself a
million excuses for doing nothing nine-tenths
of the time, but I've created a context in
which only--I realize now--only certain kinds
of feeling can come. In other words, after
all, when you've got the fort, like all the
guns mounted and ready to blast until you're
utterly safe, and you let out this little,
agonized thing . . . it skips around the room,
you know, and you're embarrassed, you hear
someone move in the kitchen, think O my God
they're *coming* . . . no wonder the poems are
short! I'm amazed that there are any at all!
At the same time, you see, one is stuck with
one's actuality, at the same time this is the
only point I can begin, this is the place
where my feelings are most present. I mean
that in the sense of I have a horrible train-
ing . . . Olson speaks of being trained to
speak, you know. He said that when he was a
younger man--he's a very large man--and as a
younger man he was . . . obviously must have
been awkward, and his presence was a problem.
He'd walk in, people would, like, duck, or
they'd *respond* to him in ways that were not
particular to his feelings at that moment. I
equally had somewhat the same thing. I found
that my feelings had an awfully bothersome
quality for people I wanted to get to. God,
I'd, you know, I'd do anything to please them,
and I found that I couldn't. I mean I couldn't
in a way that I could depend upon. So that
the poems anyhow began to be a way of dealing
with things that I was otherwise prevented from
having. Well, anyhow, a sense of security . . .
I don't mean security in the sense of insurance
or not being afraid. I think in those instances
within that room all hell breaks out, as you
well know, in the sense that everything is possible there in a way that . . . Again and
equally, if I walk on, if I'm sitting on the
train with a notebook, I'm so self-conscious

about it. Again this habit of my environment.
I think what we're trying to do with all this
is to insist to you that these aspects of what
we're talking about are not immaterial. In
other words these are the . . . I don't mean
to give them undue significance or to . . . I
don't want to qualify this way at all. What
I'm trying to say is don't start thinking of
writing as some particular activity leading to
some particular effect for some particular purpose. It is just as relevant what size paper
you use, as whether or not you think you're
writing a sonnet. In fact, it's more relevant.
And this aspect of your activity ought to be,
you ought to be aware of it, simply that you
should begin to feel as rangingly all that as
issuing as a possibility and as a qualification
of that possibility. In other words, if you
want to write with a paper like this, please
do! If you find yourself stuck with habits of
articulation, try doing something else, try
shifting the physical context . . .

[*1963*]

A Postscript

The preoccupations here evident were, in fact,
more decisive than I could then have realized.
I had trusted so much to *thinking*, apparently,
and had gained for myself such an adamant sense
of what a poem could be for me, that here I
must have been signaling to myself both a warn-
ing and the hope of an alternative.
  Not too long after I began to try deliberate-
ly to break out of the habits described. I
wrote in different states of so-called consciousness, e.g. when high, and at those times would
write in pen or pencil, contrary to habit, and
I would also try to avoid any immediate decision
as to whether or not the effects of such writing
were "good." Some of the poems so written are

to be found in *Words*, among them "A Piece,"
"The Box," "They (2)," and "The Farm." These
were, however, still written on the customary
8" by 11" sheets and in the security of my
usual home. But nonetheless they began to
gain for me the possibility of *scribbling*, of
writing for the immediacy of the pleasure and
without having to pay attention to some final
code of significance.

When *Words* was published, I was interested
to see that one of the poems most irritating
to reviewers was "A Piece"--and yet I knew
that for me it was central to all possibilities
of statement. One might think of "counting
sheep"--and I am here reminded of Williams'
poem, which Pound chooses to include in *Confucius
to Cummings*, "The High Bridge above the River
Tagus at Toledo":

> In old age they walk in the old
> man's dreams and still walk / in
> his dreams, peacefully continuing
> in his verse / forever.

To count, or give account, tell or tally, continually seems to me the occasion. But again
I had found myself limited by the nature of
the adding machine I had unwittingly forced
upon myself.

Slowly, then, I came to write without the
mechanic of the typewriter. I also began to
use notebooks, first very small ones indeed,
and then larger--and I found many senses of
possibility in writing began consequently to
open. For one, such notebooks accumulated the
writing, and they made no decisions about it--
it was all there, in whatever state it occurred,
everything from addresses to moralistic self-
advising, to such notes as I now find in the
smallest and first of them:

```
This size page forces the
damn speciously gnomic
sans need for same--
      --it
        it--
```

There was no hustle to argue the virtue of any
possibility instantly, nor to do more than
write, which same "freely" to do, as Remy de
Gourmont in Pound's quotation of him insists,
"is the sole pleasure of a writer." How long
it took me to realize that in my own life!

It would be impossible to thank Allen Ginsberg enough for what he was somehow able to
reassure me of--or to thank those other friends
whose way of writing was of like order: Robert
Duncan, Charles Olson, Denise Levertov, and the
many others, who were wise, like they say, long
before myself. It's lovely to do something
with your bare hands and mind, in the instant
it *is* possible, and finally I know it.

R.C., *April 14, 1968*

[*Audit* V:1, spring 1968]

JOHN SINCLAIR AND ROBIN
EICHELE: AN INTERVIEW
WITH ROBERT CREELEY

---

*Sinclair and Eichele talked with Creeley in
Berkeley during the University of California
Extension Division Poetry Conference, July -
August 1965. Robin Eichele taped the interview,
which was made possible by a grant from the
Miles Modern Poetry Committee of Wayne State
University.*

Eichele: Bob, I'd like you to introduce things,
to give us a brief biographical background.

Creeley: Well, it's simply done. I was born in
New England, in Arlington, Massachusetts. My
father was a doctor, and I was the younger of
two children, my sister being four years older
than me. Then he moved us out into the country,
and he died very shortly after that. My mother,
now faced with the problem of bringing us up,
went back to nursing which she'd done prior to
marrying. She was the public health nurse in
the town I really grew up in, a small sort of
farm town about 25 miles from Boston, to the
north, up past Concord: low hills, orchard country, chicken farmers and some dairy, and a rail-
road line through the center of the town, a
drug store, post office, town square, watering
trough--that kind of environment. We stayed there
pretty steadily till I was about 13 or 14, and
then we heard through my sister of a small
school and I managed to get a scholarship. So
I spent the high school years in that school in

Plymouth, New Hampshire. And then, as my sister
married and moved about in her own terms--she
married a fellow from Maine and she was very
young--I remember we moved as a family to be
near her. I don't think it was Mother's intent
to intrude on her, but I think she wanted to
be close in case there was any kind of difficulty. And then we moved to Cambridge, Massachusetts. I subsequently, after finishing high
school, went to Harvard for all but the last
of my senior year. I had married in the meantime. These were very confused years, the war
years; I can remember the constant shift and
change of the educational form trying to deal
with that stretch. They were using an accelerated program trying to rush people through before they became involved with the army. A
very chaotic time indeed. I emphasize it because it's the background for Allen Ginsberg,
myself and many of our contemporaries. The
disturbance of these years came at the end of
the Depression and the chaos of values and
assumption of values, the definition of values,
was very insistent. For example, although we
had no knowledge literally of one another,
Allen and I had many friends in common at that
time. William Cannister was perhaps the most
painfully vivid instance of one of "the best
minds of [our] generation" that one saw "des-
troyed by madness." Bill had the compulsive
need to kill himself and this need was almost
a societal condition, I mean it was almost the
actual situation of feeling in those years: a
sort of terrifying need to demonstrate the
valuelessness of one's own life. Think of the
parallel of Existentialism, for example; the
whole context of thinking in that time is incredibly self-destructive.

I went into the American Field Service in
1945 and I consequently spent a year in the
so-called India-Burma theater, driving an ambulance. So I came back sharing at least that
kind of experience with the many persons who
were returning then from the war to Harvard to

finish that scene. My friends at that time told
me a lot about things I really didn't know anything about. For example, music. I just had
had violin lessons as a kid. I never learned
to play the violin. Anyhow, I was aware that
music existed, and so when I got to college--
I'd come to college with some sense of Woody
Herman, with a general sense of what a *kind*
of music might be, but with no specific instance.
So there was the possibility of hearing what
could be more a deliberated or refined instance
of this kind of scene. It was friends in college,
for example, who first played me "Billy's Bounce"
or "Now Is the Time"--and this was a time when
Charlie Parker certainly was *present*. So all
that music became known to me and was fascinating
to me, if not in an extensive manner, still with
very actual intensity. I mean, this is the time
of the whole cult of the hipster, the forties
designation, the whole thing of being "hip" or
"with it"--when a lot of the idiom got located,
that is. "Make it," for example, is a very significant expression of that time. Things were
"the most," you know, so it was "the most" this
and "the most" that. In any case, it was a time
when one wanted desperately an intensive and an
absolutely full *experience* of whatever it was
you were engaged with. So Charlie Parker--think
of his place in Jack Kerouac's writing--became
kind of a hero of this possibility. I think of
the clubs around Boston at that time, where
frankly the kids with the background I had,
college kids, would really go and sit very god-
damned humbly, very very humbly indeed, in the
periphery of this activity. Not at all like this
sense one finds now, hanging around New Haven,
for example: I was taken to a club where the
Untouchables were playing and the college boys
of that group and that place were all but arro-
gant and I was a bit dismayed.

Sinclair: It's the same with jazz audiences now--

Creeley: Right--

Sinclair: I know; I grew up with that, must
have been a nineteen-forties sensibility and
when I first started to hear jazz I would go
to a club and sit and hope I might get to meet
a musician.

Creeley: Audiences were really very humble at
that time, especially if they felt they didn't
have means for an immediate response. This is
significant: John Chamberlain, the sculptor,
whose first wife is a black girl, a singer,
and John had the same appetite to get it on;
he came from Rochester, Indiana. Everyone was
looking for where it was happening and desperately wanted to be accepted by it, because
frankly the society as it then was, coming
back from the war and realizing home and mother
just wasn't, no matter how lovely, any great
possibility. And equally the fade-out of the
whole sense of being *professional*: trying to
become a doctor, a lawyer, the value of one's
life as a progression toward some attention
was gone because the war demonstrated that no
matter how much you tried, as Morganthau said:
facts have their own dynamic--and this could
never be anticipated by any form of adjustment.
Anyhow, so those were the years that I began
to hear jazz for the first time, of this kind,
Charlie Parker and the whole range of those
very, to my mind, significant people.
   Thelonious Monk, of course, is the kind of
man who not only survived but continued right
through this whole period. And, as I say, drum-
mers like Max Roach and those early groups,
which one wouldn't want to do without, Al Haig,
for example. Jacky Byard was then playing in
Boston. Dick Twardzik was another brilliant
pianist from Boston; he was with a group when
he would have been 14, or something like that,
in 1946--like men who couldn't play on union
terms but could pick up a gang of teenage kids
and have bands, really--I wish I could remember
the names of them. I remember the first time I
ever saw Dick Twardzik: he was sitting on a

piano stool that he could barely reach from,
this gangly kid with this dead-set face and
utter composure. I mean you could tell from
his dress he had nothing else he could offer
but his ability to play the piano. He could
probably not articulate any other part of his
identity,but that piano was really what he
knew and so here he would be with this blond-
maned character, I wish I could remember his
name, a Stan Kenton type, you know, *hope*, played
this golden trumpet--

Sinclair: Pomeroy? Was it Herb Pomeroy?

Creeley: No, it wasn't him. But it was someone
who would really collect this gang of emaciated
kids and make, you know, fantastic sounds. Then
there were places like the High Hat which is
now a garage and gas station, and the Club Savoy,
I think it was called.
    So there was an interesting flux in jazz.
One of my first friends was a young trumpet
player, Joe Leach, from around Detroit and he
came to Cambridge, to go to college--and he
told me an awful lot about jazz without, you
know, *telling* me. I think he was doing the same
job you have, John, for *Downbeat* for a time.
I remember his family were old-time Dixieland
people who wanted to keep their kids out of it,
you know, and all three children managed to
learn to play whatever it was interested them
with the family's absolute disagreement. That's
sort of random but I want to give some sense
of that time. This is what I was doing from
1946 to 1950. I was frankly doing almost nothing else but sitting around listening to records,
which my first wife would be pleased to testify
to. I listened to records. I was *fascinated* by
them; well, first of all, not at all easily,
I was fascinated with what these people did
with *time*. Not to impose this kind of intellectual term upon it, as I'd question that; but I
want to emphasize this was where I was hearing
"things said" in terms of rhythmic and sound

possibilities--you see, Auden was the alternative if one was depending on reading. But I
should make clear Henry Miller was the hero
of these years, Kenneth Patchen was the hero
of these years, D.H. Lawrence was the hero of
these years, Hart Crane--they were the people
who kept saying that something *is* possible,
it's possible to *say* something, you really
have access to your feelings and can really
use them as a demonstration of your own reality. You can write directly from that which you
feel, and these musicians made clear how *subtle*
and how sophisticated, not simply sophisticated
as a kind of social label, but how *refined* that
expression might be. I think that's what really
attracted me to them; they were *not* dumb. I
don't think I could ever be interested in dumb-
ness as a way of life. In fact, how to keep
alive was so much involved with how sharp you
could be. So these were those times: the same
man who played the first Charlie Parker record
I ever heard was the same man who gave me the
first book of Ezra Pound's that I read.

Sinclair: That's the same experience I had.
The guy laid *Howl* on me.

Creeley: I married the last of my time in college; I married say the last of my junior year
and survived the first of my senior year and
then quit. At that time I had friends local to
the college scene: the people I really feel
significant in that sense, not as influences
upon me in an obvious way but friends, as Jack
Hawkes, the novelist--he was really a key
figure for me at that time--I knew, for example,
Kenneth Koch and *liked* him but I had no real
intimacy with him of any kind.
   There was a group centered around a magazine
called *Wake*, which began almost as a demonstration that the *Harvard Advocate* was not to be
the only possibility for writing at the college,
which was so vast that no one knew what it was,
anyhow. Thousands of people. So *Wake* was our

protest of our exclusion from that possibility.
I should also say I later became a very suspect member of the *Harvard Advocate*. At the
time it was really never thought to exist, and
was subsequently closed almost immediately by
the actions of another musician friend, actually from Cleveland; he began to take drugs,
so he began taking books out of the *Advocate*
library, which had signed Eliot editions, etc.,
to sell them, you know. I could only watch in
fascination. It seemed to me that they were
fairly useless things that he was getting rid
of, and I, you know, it was an instance of
property, I was still worrying about *whose*
books they were and really would continue to
but Jack didn't really care about whose books
they were. So at that time I had these kinds
of friends. Then I married and moved to Provincetown, really on the strength of a friendship with the first writer I ever knew, a man
named Slater Brown, who was sort of down on
his luck at that time, who is happily not at
all involved with such problems presently.
He was extremely generous with me; he had
been a close friend of both Cummings (he is
the B in *The Enormous Room*) and Hart Crane,
in fact, one of the few people consistently
sympathetic to Crane's situation. Crane had
many supporters all through his life but they
often became curiously critical of him, people
who really liked him for his vitality and
intelligence but then began to be all hung up
with his conduct. He was not an easy man to be
friends with, apparently. In any case, Slater
listened to me, not just as my rambling then
might have gone on, but he paid me the respect
of taking me seriously in my own intentions.
He was a very good friend indeed. So we moved
to Provincetown and lived there about a year.

I should note, because it's relevant, that
I wasn't working during these years; I had no
job. We were living on the income that my wife
had from her trust fund, a small amount of
money that really postponed the actual engage-

ment with how *do* you live in the world. The
novel I've written, *The Island*, really gives
the content of those years. It isn't the story
of my life but it makes much use of that time.
In any case, I had all during this time no
real sense of being a writer in any way; it
was just an imaginative possibility that I
really wanted to try to get to. I mean I wanted to write desperately; I wanted that to be
it. But at the same time I couldn't demonstrate
any competence in it. The connection with Jack
Hawkes led me to being published in the issues
of *Wake* that he was involved with. But it was
a long time before I had an active nucleus of
people I worked particularly in relation to--
as, for example, Olson or Blackburn, who was
my first acquaintance with this kind of person. That chance hearing of Cid Corman's program on the Boston station led to many relationships. By that time we had moved from just
outside Provincetown to New Hampshire where
we had a kind of rundown farm and I remember
we were endlessly trying to repair the house.

We had this plan of having a garden, which
we did have, and it gave us potatoes and corn
and beans and all that. I was absorbed with
pigeons and chickens; I was really fascinated
by both of them. I was raising a variety of
breeds and I had a very good friend at that
time named Ira Grant,who any breeder of Barred
Rocks would remember; he was a very very, you
know, *great* old man. I learned more about
poetry as an actual activity from raising
chickens than I did from any professor at the
university. I learned more from this chicken
farmer about how do you pay attention to
things. He had no embarrassment confronting
his own attention. He did not try to distract
you with something else. It's stupidly placed
perhaps in this situation and context, but I
one time wrote to a man named Charles Schultz
in Lincolnwood, Illinois, about a particular
pigeon he had raised that won a national award
as a grand champion, a big competitive possibility,

and I wrote to him about this particular bird.
I'd seen its picture and it was really a lovely pigeon, a lovely thing, and I said how did
you breed it, what's the breeding on the bird,
and this letter came back with painstaking
script, that sort of lovely old man's handwriting, a farmer's handwriting somehow and,
you know, *my dear sir, my dear Mr. Creeley,*
whatever, with the address and all this business and then followed, "In 19--" (I can't
remember the exact year) the letter began like,
"In 1908 I secured from so-and-so at such-and-
such a place two pairs of such-and-such a pigeon."
And he gave the history of that bird, and I
thought, God, this is more serious than anything anyone ever said to me in the university.
I didn't know this is the patience that's necessary.

That sort of circumstance taught me a lot
more than what I was previously involved with.
In the meantime obviously I was reading and
had happily good occasion to, but I was embarrassed to find out at times how involved I was
with poultry, and yet these men curiously al-
lowed me *all* my enthusiasm. I mean, take the
Red Pigmy Pouters, which I bred: all the dominant terms in judging this bird for exhibition
are based on *recessive* characteristics. I mean
almost every feature of this bird, the distin-
guishing marks which are used in its judging,
are almost all without exception recessive:
its globe, the way the bird stands, the length
of its legs, even the color, the characteristics
to which these breeders give attention are almost all recessive--like the *red* color, that's
a recessive color for these birds, and it's
very interesting that this should have been
the color for the grand champion of that year.

Eichele: That was when?

Creeley: The late forties.

Eichele: Took about forty years to put it
together--

Creeley: Yeah. This was a young bird, literally a young cock, and this means the bird is
one year or younger. There are two classes for
age in shows: young bird and old bird; "old
bird" is anything over a year old. Well, after
the first molt, they molt once, but the characteristics of the color particularly, and the
feathering, can change very drastically in
that molt so that a young bird of this kind
might be useless in another year as a show
bird. So they also taught me the fragility of
the situation, these people, and they also
taught what can matter, you see, so many of
us are concerned with the significance of our
activities; that is, I think a lot of people
have a common embarrassment, one might say,
in thinking of poems as an actual thing they
might engage their attention with because they
say it doesn't count, and what does a poem
have to do with the world, I mean it's very
interesting to read and feel this man's emotions concerning this or that situation but
this doesn't, you know, pay the gas bill--but
you see these men with their pigeons cut through
all that and, god, they were a lovely range
of person: they go all the way from literally
multi-multi-millionaires like Edgar Ball, who
would give up a cattle show where he was showing his prize cows, would give up the possibility of going there to come to Boston to watch
the judging of the Bald Head Tumblers, you
know, *or* equally the man who might live in
Boston, Massachusetts, and who had just a small
coop out back and this was his scene too--so,
frankly, there was a lovely democracy you see,
because all that really meant anything was the
particular bird and that bird *did* have or perhaps not simple parallel but actual parallel
with the circumstances in poetry: it was human
attention given to the possibilities of human
life. The bird was as perishable, as fleeting
and as useless as anything can be--I mean, god,
the Pigmy Pouter is of no use to anyone in the
sense that you don't make any money from it.

No one, I'm sure, makes a living from raising
pigeons unless they're for the public market
in the sense of food.

Sinclair: And how much pigeon can you eat?

Creeley: Not too much--

Eichele: Did the situation occur that sometimes
does happen in, say, cattle shows; the grand
champion being sold for fantastic amounts of
money for a stud?

Creeley: No, because that's another interesting thing about pigeons. A bird that gets to
be a champion is a *show bird*; it's a very careful vocabulary. But then you have what are
called *stock birds* and stock birds are the
birds that are used, frankly, in breeding show
birds. Stock birds may have overemphasized
characteristics. Then you do get into genetics.
But a stock bird is a very distinct bird in
that it is used in breeding the qualifications,
the qualities you want to have in breeding a
bird that will then be used for show. But a
show bird is oftentimes of no use as a breeder
at all. I mean, he's just a moment in time. I
remember one instance of pigeons I was given
as a kid--I had an interest early--a pair of
fantails, a very common bird around New England.
Once you got past icehouse pigeons, the pigeons
you could get by climbing up into icehouses or
whatever they nest in, and taking the young
two or three week old birds out of the nests,
getting young *squeakers* as they call them--
once you get past that you then went to homing
pigeons, *homers* we used to call them, or fan-
tails--these were very common varieties. Well,
this one pair of fantails I was given suddenly
bred a fantastically good fantail. But I was
a kid; I didn't know anything about banding,
and you can't show birds without having them
banded; that's part of the etiquette in the
show scene. This bird was what we call a sport;

he was suddenly a lucky strike in the genetic
situation. But I mean that taught me to pay
attention to a lot of things. I'm surprised
now; I haven't been engaged with pigeons for
almost fifteen or more years--almost twenty
years now--and yet the habits of that attention as we're now talking is so precise that
they give me the vocabulary immediately. I
mean, I couldn't tell you the same kind of
detail about the method of scanning a line
of poetry or various systems of metric that
are involved with descriptions of poetry. Now
I found that one information was useful and
felt right in my environment; not that I wanted to be only a pigeon man but I mean that
kind of information taught me a lot. It taught
me how to pay attention to an awful lot of
things.

So, that would really occupy the years up
till about 1950. And the house we were then
living in in New Hampshire had been a problem
for us; we were unable to keep up payments;
we had had a very unhappy event, one of our
children had died; so we were emotionally, like
they say, anxious to be somewhere else. The
continual problem of keeping the property not
so much *private* but--there was a pool, a rock
pool, a river formed a lovely basin, and it was
a lovely place to swim, about the only place
that was easily got to for this neighborhood.
And we had no problem with the people living
with us in the sense of the intimate friends
or even the acquaintances--but we had this
awful business of random tourists. The motels,
for instance, began to send people there to
swim. So one day I remember walking down the
road and realizing that a traveling carnival
had taken all their rubbish and just dumped
it in this woods. That kind of irritation just
got frustrating. Anyhow, we were in the mood
to leave. And I had met, through a classmate
like they say at Harvard, Mitchell Goodman,
he's a novelist, I happened to meet his wife,
who is Denise Levertov. They'd gone to live

in France on the G.I. Bill that Mitch could
get money from. We were anxious to move and
we thought, well, living in Europe, the basic
small income that my wife had would probably
allow us to be more comfortable. So we went
to France on that basis and we lived as neighbors of the Goodmans', say in fifty, fifty-one
--and then they moved off. We stayed in France
for about three years and we had a very difficult time there. We had hit a time of infla-
tion so that our money, the availability of
what we had to spend, was very much restricted. We had two children by that time, and a
third child was born there.

Then through the coincidence of little magazines, which is frankly why we're all here,
the coincidence of literary relationships--I
came into contact with a young poet, an Englishman, who had published a poem in a magazine
that struck me very much, not so much in his
technique but in the feelings. He was still
using the habitual modes of traditional verse.
He was a man named Martin Seymour Smith. And
I wrote to him care of the magazine to say
that poem, you know, was very interesting and
it turned out that he was working as tutor
for Robert Graves' son William in Mallorca.
This was a curious job. William Merwin had
been the man who had the job just before him.
Anyhow, we got into correspondence and I would
complain in the letters about the difficulties
of living in France, the kind of unsettledness:
there was a great political criticism of Americans in France at that time. He said, why don't
you come here, and he and his wife then came
to pay us a visit in France, and I sort of returned with them with the idea that I look
over the scene and see where we might live. So
we moved to Mallorca. Actually the origin of
the Divers Press is really due to Martin because he had a program underway to publish
books. And Martin, like they say, had a mother
who was very anxious to see herself in print.
Her actual name was Mrs. Frank Seymour Smith,

which was Martin's father, who was one of the most able bookmen for W.H. Smith and Sons in England. He had a knowledge of books as objects; he was neither a critic nor a literary man but he knew books as actual things and had his own concerns with them. But he was very humble about literature. Any man who loves books is humble about literature. But Martin had got involved with the politics of literature. Staying around Graves you do. Graves is very ingenuous in many ways and is, you know, not really very interested in manipulating the possibilities, he certainly wasn't in those years, but at the same time he is very involved with literary activity as *person*. So anyhow we moved to Mallorca and we started this press and I could see very quickly that neither Martin nor myself was going to agree to any sense the other had of what the format, what the look of the book should be. I think we published one, possibly two books--then I split off and my wife and I continued to print books using the Divers Press as a name. I also had the relation now with *Origin*--*Origin* starts 1950, 1951--the first issue is Charles Olson, and happily the second issue, my stories, and so forth.

Sinclair: This is curious to me: how much did you publish before the second issue of *Origin*?

Creeley: I had published in magazines that had no continuity. I mean, they were mostly random. *Wake*, for example, had no continuity. It stopped and then there was nothing that picked up on its occasion. I was writing to Paul Carroll recently, who was reminiscing about *Big Table*. Now *Big Table* picks up on the fact that *Origin* is not being printed further, that *Black Mountain Review* is starting to peter out, that *Evergreen* is becoming very public. *Big Table* picks up on the impulse of the whole possibility. But then there are magazines--I don't even want to give them names--not that I don't

like them, but they're things like *Wings* or
Dedicated or *Here* (*Here* is actually more interesting; there is a magazine called *Here*)
but I was published in magazines that I don't
like, like *The Window*, or magazines that are
continuing because of the persistence of the
editor but have no idea of literary continuity. But I think, all told, I could not have
published more than a dozen poems. I was writing a lot but I was not publishing. I mean,
say a friend says, we'd like some poems, so
you send *all* the poems you possess and they
take, reasonably, two pages. Then there are
the difficulties with the printer and with
the money; so if a magazine makes it, it usually comes out six to eight months after your
initial intention. And that's because everybody was stuck with the *physical* problem of
getting work into print. I can remember Richard Emerson and Fred Eckman were editing a
magazine called *Golden Goose* which had a continuity, and they printed my first book [*Le Fou*]
actually in their series; they also printed
Williams' *The Pink Church*, for example. They
printed [Norman] MacCleod. They were very sympathetic to Patchen. And interested in Pound.
They were a contemporary coherence. They took
a book of Charles Olson's called *The Praises*.
This actually got into proof. Then there was
a falling out among them and the book never
was printed, never was run off. Then subsequently that book becomes *In Cold Hell, In
Thicket*; Cid Corman's *Origin* took over that
for its eighth issue and gave the book, which
was now changed a bit, that title. But what
I'm trying to get to here, is that at this
time there is a kind of exploration of these
relationships. And they begin to accumulate.
A knows B, B knows C, and there begins to be
increasing focus. And I think we were curiously lucky that that focus was not literally a
question of whether we were all living together
or not. You know, people get married and go
off about their business; if they have a

relationship that depends upon being present
to one another, physically, then it's pretty
difficult to sustain. Because circumstances
lead people to other scenes. But that relationship among those writers who are identified as the *Origin* group never was complicated
by a literal geography. Almost all those
people were managing their relationships
through the mails. That was a time of intense
letter writing. For example, I can remember
the time that Olson went to Yucatan and the
material that I collected then in *Mayan Letters*.
And this book must be no more than a fourth
or possibly less of the number of letters he
was writing. He used to write so that letters
were coming in five times a week. And they
were long, you know--

Sinclair: And he was writing to other people
all along--

Creeley: Right! He was continually in a process
of this kind with everyone. And these were
really very intensive statements about what
was concerning him then and there. It was sort
of an unconscious newsletter of his own concerns. At this same time he was involved with
Shakespeare. There's happily a lovely essay
as yet unpublished called "Quantity in Verse
and Shakespeare's Late Plays." It's going to
be collected now in this *Human Universe* volume.
It's a lovely demonstration of what he was
thinking of and it's an extremely useful piece
of writing; he also spoke a lot about what the
condition of language was in a *sequence*, call
it prose or poetry. So there was Shakespeare,
and he was also very involved with the Civil
War; he was still involved with the issue both
politically and dynamically of the context of
the U.S. after the Second World War. You remember he worked for the Democratic Party. He
was I think chairman to the foreign language
groups represented at the Democratic Conven-
tion, during Roosevelt's administration. He

comes into that context of persons Roosevelt
hired as experts in divers particular disciplines. I mean, I think Roosevelt was the first
man to formalize the context of expert advice,
which was already well known in business. And
in the persons that he thus assembled, you
have people like Oppenheimer. And you also
have Owen Lattimore. I mean, these were persons chosen for their particular experience,
rather than their political or social form.

Eichele: When did you start corresponding with
Olson?

Creeley: I think it was about 1948 or 1949. I
hate to give you an exact date. It follows
from Cid: Cid knew Vincent Ferrini, Vincent
Ferrini sent some poems to me--we were trying
to start a magazine which subsequently was
absorbed by *Origin*; we couldn't get the printing done. We didn't have the money nor the
means.

Sinclair: Was there much of a commitment to
that activity by that time?

Creeley: Oh, yeah. It's the dissatisfaction
with the social occasion of writing. Not that
we didn't like it, we didn't have a background
for it. You see, aspects of that *kind* of writing and its people do continue very actively
in Kenneth Koch's and Frank O'Hara's work on
the one hand, or in Donald Hall's work--Hall
was also at Harvard--they continued in the
social situation of writers. Not that they
were the less writers, but they had a use of
it socially that we didn't have. Bunny Lang's
--V.R. Lang's--ability to be so active in
the Actors' Workshop group in Cambridge, is
part of her whole *social* situation. I mean,
she made I think very interesting use of it.
But this was a social possibility that writers
as myself didn't have. Really we were from
the other side of the tracks almost. I remember

one time, a classic meeting: I was taken down
to a cafe, you know I was still about 26, perhaps 27, and I went down with *my* gang, I mean
I was very humble in my pleasure in being admitted into the group that was centered as
Merlin. There was Alexander Trocchi, there
was Pat Bowles, who interestingly became editor of *The Paris Review*, because Pat Bowles,
who was the rough tough kid from South Africa,
had the *professional* ability to edit a magazine. You see now *The Paris Review*, not to
castigate them socially, but they were all
the kids who went to Harvard who came from
good families. These were kids that all moved
in a social milieu that did not permit us. So
I remember walking into that cafe with Alex
and all the dead-end kids of my association
and we were sitting down and here across the
tables were these, you know, these comfortably
and sort of shyly aggressive young men, all
of good breeding and manners, who were the
editors of *The Paris Review*, with their wives
and children sort of making a post F. Scott
Fitzgerald business. Whereas Alex, I remember,
used to almost check the arriving boat lists
to see what available young American ladies
might be found to con into putting money into
his magazine. He and the others literally
used to sit down (I've been present at such
decisions) to decide which among them would
be most attractive to the young American who
had just wandered into such and such a bar,
so that they could con her. And they'd con
her in the name of art, as I would con anybody in the name of art, if I could accept
my own behavior. In any case, they weren't
just going out and lushing; god, it was very
severe--I mean these men were *not* self-indul-
gent. Just witness their activity. They were
the first significant publishers of Beckett,
for example; they were the first significant
publishers in English of Genet. Collection
Merlin, if you look at the titles, shows the
whole foundation of Barney Rosset's subsequent
activity.

So in any case, *that* was a happy relationship.
This was all happening in the fifties as we
began to become identified as active in some
literary way, because attention began to come.
This had nothing to do with making money or
anything. We began to realize ourselves, to
get location, to realize what other writers
were particular to our own discriminations.
Gerhardt in Germany I felt very much for in
this sense. In England we were really unable
to find anyone; I don't think we ever did at
that time. We now begin to. There's a magazine published by Brian Patton, called *Underdog*. There are many magazines. There's *Out-
burst*, for example, edited by Tom Raworth.
And see now the college crowd is beginning
to pick up on the possibility, as witness the
issues of *Granta*, and even *The Isis* now, begin to show some life.

Sinclair: What about *Prospect*?

Creeley: Yes, *Prospect* is interesting. That's
a magazine published at Cambridge, edited by
Jeremy Prynne, a teaching fellow, I think,
and a very, very good bibliographer and a
poet also. But that's a traditional under-
graduate magazine that has had a kind of
separation from the traditional scene; it's
usually picked up by the discontents, you know,
as a way of getting hold of something they
can think about. That's how that letter to
Elaine Feinstein came about; she just wrote
Olson and said: what are you doing? And Charles
wrote this pretty impressive suggestion of
what language might be thought of as doing:
something you track into your own experience
of it, but also have the possibility of track-
ing in its own environment as it *has* had an
existence. So you test it, as he says, in and
out. And words, when they're so received or
felt, become really very interesting.

Eichele: Could we turn now to the Black Mountain

situation, how you got involved?

Creeley: Let's see. I'm at this point living
in Mallorca. And I'm having, like they say,
this intensive, continuing correspondence with
Olson. *Origin* has now been going on for some
years; it's not tired but it's really been
carrying a lot of weight for some time. And
I think too that we do begin to define our
intentions, and some of us begin to feel not
a separation but increasing qualification.
We become impatient with some of the things
done and wish more might be done about others.
So we begin to feel there is room for two
magazines, not as a criticism at all of Cid's
--he is the coherence, always has been--but
we begin to think we have enough going for
two. And also, Charles was interested--he was
now in the position of Rector at Black Mountain
--and he was interested to think of some way
money might most effectively be used for some
activity. That is, the college was now embarrassed in the sense that many, many people
were not even aware that it existed, so to
hope to get enough students to support its
activity was in that way hopeful indeed. We
one time literally sat down and figured out
with pencil and paper that if we had 35 students we could be self-supporting, and we were
unable, we were embarrassed to get 35 students
in 1955. So, Charles figured that a magazine
--and 35 people are not a large number--a
magazine could conceivably get to 35 interested
persons.
I was very close to Charles through letters
but I had not even met him at the time *The
Black Mountain Review* was being planned. So
he was involved with *that* business. And he
thought, well, if the college published a
magazine, this would be the best use of the
money available for publicizing itself. That
really would effectively distribute the fact
that the college was alive; he said, it's like
a flag: that's the best way to haul it up. So

anyhow, he thereby undertook to get me I think
it was about $400 an issue. Or some amount like
that. He covered the cost of the issue, in
short. We printed four or five hundred copies.
And that's the way it happened to be published
spring, 1954, from Mallorca. And then there
was an attempt to interest people we thought
perhaps might be. Paul Goodman had taught at
Black Mountain, for example. He said, I don't
want to be a contributing editor but I'm sympathetic to what you're doing, and I don't want
to take on any concern with what you're doing
in a responsible way but I will be willing to
help in any other way I can. Kenneth Rexroth
did come on as a contributing editor but he
was very soon offended because we published
two articles: one, criticizing Dylan Thomas
and the other criticizing Theodore Roethke--
and in those days neither man was criticized.
Really we were criticizing the critics of
these people; we were criticizing them for
making such a structure of assumption about
the activity of either of these two men. It
was as though Thomas was *only* approachable
through this great wash of sentimental regard
for his ability to read poems while dead drunk.
There's a great love of *that* possibility, the
Falstaffian figure. And I thought it became
a vulgarization of the whole actuality of his
words, of *the* words--they're not his, he didn't
make them. And the second thing was that Roethke
had become sort of the American Dylan Thomas.
Anyhow Kenneth didn't want to be embarrassed
in his own associations.

And then Charles invited me to come teach
at Black Mountain, which I'd really never considered myself doing. I wasn't a teacher: I
didn't know how to teach. But I was desperate
to get out of Mallorca so I took him up on it.
And boy, with great tentativeness I went. And
the persons I met there that first time! I
went, actually, twice; I stayed there for perhaps three to four months, then went back to
Mallorca, spent almost another year and then

returned again--after the breakup of my marriage,
and that's best left in the novel. That first
time, Mike Rumaker was there; he was very significant for me. Ed Dorn was there; he was
significant for me. I felt that these persons
were very *very* interesting indeed. One was primarily a prose writer, the other was writing
both prose and poetry and he was such a lovely,
resistant *man*--he didn't accept anything on
faith; he tested all of his experiences just
in order to make sure that he was there too.
He didn't want to take it away for himself
but he wanted to make sure he had offered it
a significant recognition. He never takes
things easily. So he was there. And then Charles
of course was there. It was a lovely company
of persons, no matter how difficult the circumstance of survival. And so I found something
I had never expected to find: an actual educational organization that was depending upon
the authority of its teaching, not on any assumption about that teaching. The college was
operated by the faculty. The faculty owned
it. The students were completely open; there
was very little qualification offered them
as to their coming in. There was a very intensive program, but it didn't have the usual
formality. It wasn't simply a question of being to class on time, or where is Anthropology
102 meeting this week, or anything of that
kind; it was intensely preoccupied with *how*
teaching is accomplished, in all of its aspects.
And therefore it came to feel it is much more
relevant to have a man who has intimate association with some activity as its possible in-
structor. Not to tell you the story of my life,
but it's much better to be hanging around a
blacksmith's shop if you want to learn how to
make horseshoes than to be reading books about
them.

Sinclair: How about people like Jonathan Williams, Wieners--

Creeley: Jonathan was a student there. I met him actually first in Mallorca. He'd been in the Army. And he came to visit us in Mallorca --but he was known to me, we were known to one another primarily through Black Mountain and Charles. Then John Wieners I remember first meeting at Black Mountain. I've always been deeply touched that John Wieners' first acquaintance with his own possibility as a poet was because Charles read in Boston--I think it was the Trinity Church, which is a sort of old-fashioned church that has civic activities-- and Charles for some reason was invited to read there. And it happened that John Wieners was in the audience. He was going to do something else that evening but he just happened to stop in and listen--

Eichele: And he also got a copy of *The Black Mountain Review*--

Creeley: Yes, Charles had copies of *Black Mountain Review* #1 that he was passing out. He was *pitching*; I mean he wanted to demonstrate that his college had an active possibility. Anyhow, I happened to be there when John came down for a visit.

Sinclair: He was one of the 35.

Creeley: Yeah. And I drove back to New York with him--well, he was on the way to Boston. Charles and myself and I can't quite remember who else was present, I think there were one or two other people and John and Dana--we drove back in the car. So we had an acquaintance. John was very quiet in those days; he had a lovely sort of tentative manner--he just wanted to look around. He was a very courteous man.

Eichele: What happened as a group to bring these people together who had been carrying on this intense correspondence?

Creeley: That really never *did* happen. That is,
all the persons were not ever really together
with one another. I remember in Vancouver a
couple of years ago, Charles or Robert or somebody said, gee, this is the first time that
we've all been together. It was really the first
time in our lives that the three of us were
present at the same time. In other words, Robert
had spent a short period in Mallorca; I'd met
him there first, he'd come over--through *Origin*
we were known to each other. Robert had wanted
to be in Mallorca, he wrote me because he knew
it was cheap to live there, and we helped him
find a house. Denise and I had been together
both in the States and in France; Paul and I
had known each other in New York; Paul came
to Mallorca. Olson I'd known at Black Mountain.
But I mean we *weren't* a nucleus geographically
ever. Although Robert also taught at Black
Mountain he came, I think, literally when I
left. The second time. He stayed on till the
college finished. Or at least had to close
because of lack of money. But it's almost more
interesting to demonstrate that the *place* can
be as viable as this then was, that this activity of coming and going is relevant to education also because what contemporary education
is facing is the problem that it has an increasingly static or unwieldy *location*. Colleges
can't be *put* in the country; they can't be *put*
in the city. You've demonstrated that a college
occurs--I'm thinking, John and Robin, of your
own activity with the Artist's Workshop--
you're demonstrating that a college occurs at
any point that this concern of how do you
measure, how is value possible, how do you
have the use of yourself in what activity you
do--any time this is admitted as a context a
college occurs. It's what Alex Trocchi is now
talking about with his sense of *spontaneous
university*. Now see this is really a dilemma
because I remember visiting at Michigan State
and talking to various friends there, people
I'd met there, and they said, the courses aren't

really the problem--the actual physical organization of the place is almost overwhelming:
35,000 students and we're not worried about
who will teach *Beowulf*, we're worried about
how do you keep that plumbing from breaking
down. This kind of problem is immense, really
immense indeed--literally so.

But this college that we had in mind was as
viable and as momentary and as moving as the
fact that people moved around in their lives.
The different attentions at different moments
in time. So it was a place to *go*. It really
was that place we were talking about apropos
this conference: a place to go sit down when
you wanted to. And we weren't limited: people
were always drifting through, coming back,
coming for the first time. And the very form
that Olson insisted upon for his own teaching
there when he first came to Black Mountain
was that he would come down at the end of each
month and stay perhaps four or five days and
work intensively with people, then go back to
Washington where he'd been living and go
about his own business; I mean he not only
knew, he realized entirely that you don't get
anything from someone who's not given time to
be active; you can't get anything from a
painter who's prepared to sit in a classroom
talking *about* painting all day. He's just not
going to be able to do the thing. You certainly can't find out anything from a man who's
active in some context if he's not given the
opportunity of doing what he literally can do.

[*Whe're* 1, summer 1966]

LINDA W. WAGNER: A
COLLOQUY WITH
ROBERT CREELEY

---

*It is impossible to know Robert Creeley and
his work without being convinced that he is
one of the most honest men alive, and one of
the most intense. Both qualities are evident
in his scrupulous exactness; no effort is too
great for his work, and for its acknowledged
purpose, to please others as well as himself.
His writing is notable for its painstaking--
and sometimes painful--clarity and accuracy.
In today's somewhat romantic artistic milieu,
Creeley thrives on the process of coming to
terms, on definition. As a case in point, his
often quoted definition of* form *as "an extension of content"; or, here, the word* colloquy
*used as a description of what I had termed an
interview. Creeley corrected me, defining both
words and insisting on* colloquy *because my
questions were "active in their own assumptions
. . . . we've made distinctions, we are talking together insofar as you are obviously
stimulating me to senses of things that I'm
trying to get clear and equally, I hope, this
can be a two-way process. It's impossible that
a man should be only 'a fact in himself' and
there only for interview, as if the interviewer
were not a part of the process, in an active
form indeed." And so this colloquy with Robert
Creeley, begun in spirit at the 1963 Vancouver
poetry sessions; continued at his 1964 Bowling
Green, Ohio, reading; and crystallized in New
Mexico, August, 1965.* L.W.W.

Wagner: You have said that poetry is "the basic
act of speech, of utterance." Are you implying
that self-expression is the poet's motivation,
or is there more to be said about his desire
to communicate, his interest in possible readers?

Creeley: I don't think that "possible readers"
are really the context in which poetry is written. For myself it's never been the case. I'm
looking for something I can say--I'm not looking for a job or an easy solution to problems
--but I'm given to write as I can and in that
act I use whatever I can to gain the articulation that seems to me called for. And I certainly will pay no attention to possible readers
insofar as they may not respond to what I've
offered in this way. I have found, for example,
that the poems I wrote in the fifties, which
at that time had only the sympathetic reading
of friends, that those poems have gained the
audience here implied, not because I intended
it but simply because I have gained them--but
I could never have anticipated that. If one in
that way plays to the gallery, I think it's
extraordinarily distracting. The whole performance of writing then becomes some sort of odd
entertainment of persons one never meets and
probably would be embarrassed to meet in any
case. So I'm only interested in what I can
articulate with the things given me as confron-
tation. I can't worry about what it costs me.
I don't think any man writing can worry about
what the act of writing costs him, even though
at times he is very aware of it. Again, when
Stendhal dedicated his work in effect to readers
who would be alive--in say 1930, 1935, a hundred
years later--he recognized the political and
social circumstances that would make him politically suspect; so that he obviously wrote for
the sheer pleasure and relief of the articulation so to be gained. And I would say, I do too.

Wagner: Communication *per se*, then, isn't a primary motive for the poet?

Creeley: It is for some; for others, it isn't.
It depends on what is meant by communication,
of course. I, for example, would be very much
cheered to realize that someone had felt what
I had been feeling in writing--I would be very
much reassured that someone had felt with me
in that writing. Yet this can't be the context
of my own writing. When I come to write, I
frankly cannot be distracted by what people are
going to think of what I'm writing. Later I may
have horrible doubts indeed as to what it is
and whether or not it will ever be read with
this kind of response by other persons, but
it can never enter importantly into my writing.

So, I cannot say that communication in the
sense of telling someone is what I'm engaged
with. In writing I'm telling something to myself, curiously, that I didn't have the knowing of previously. One time, again some years
ago, Franz Kline was being questioned--not
with hostility but with intensity, by another
friend--and finally he said, "Well, look, if
I paint what *you* know, then that will simply
bore you, the repetition from me to you. If I
paint what *I* know, it will be boring to myself.
Therefore I paint what I *don't* know." And I
write what I don't know, in that sense.

Communication, then, is a word one would
have to spend much time defining. One question
I have--doesn't all speech imply that one is
speaking with what is known, is possible of
discovery? "Can you tell someone something he
doesn't know?" has always been a question in
my own mind. And if it is true that you cannot
tell someone something "new," then the act of
reading is that one is reading *with* someone.
And I feel that when people read my poems most
sympathetically, they are reading with me as
I am writing with them. So communication this
way is mutual feeling with someone, not a didactic process of information.

Wagner: I have increasingly felt that to some
poets--Allen Ginsberg, William Carlos Williams,

yourself--this being read *with*, sympathetically, was very important.

Creeley: There are many, many ways of feeling in the world, and many qualifications of that feeling. At times in my own life I've been embarrassed to feel I had a significant rela- tionship with other people--that is, I felt that my world was extraordinarily narrow and egocentric and possible only to some self- defined importance. So that reading in that sense I've just spoken of--that sympathetic being with--has always been an important pos- sibility for me. What Robert Duncan calls the ideal reader has always been someone I've thought of--but not *in* writing, *after* it.

Wagner: One question that's fairly relevant here might be this issue of using so-called prose rhythms in poetry, of taking the language of poetry from natural speech. How does the poet himself decide what is poetry and what is conversation? And are they as close as the theory seems to indicate?

Creeley: If we think of Louis Zukofsky's poetics as being "a function with upper limit music and lower limit, speech," perhaps that will help to clarify what the distinctions are. Really, the organization of poetry has moved to a fur- ther articulation in which the rhythmic and sound structure now becomes not only evident but a primary coherence in the total organi- zation of what's being experienced. In conver- sation, you see, this is not necessarily the case. It largely isn't, although people speak- ing (at least in American speech) do exhibit clusters or this isochronous pattern of phrase groups with one primary stress; so there is a continuing rhythmic insistence in conversa- tion. But this possibility has been increased in poetry so that now the rhythmic and sound organization have been given a very marked emphasis in the whole content. Prose rhythms

in poetry are simply one further possibility
of articulating pace; these so-called prose
rhythms tend to be slower so that therefore
they give perhaps a useful drag.

I would like to make the point that it
isn't that poets are using "common" words or
a common vocabulary. This kind of commonness
is deceptive. For example, if one reads Williams carefully, he finds that the words are
not largely common. What is common is the *mode*
of address, the way of speaking that's commonly
met with in conversations. But when that occurs
in poetry, already there's a shift that is
significant: that fact in a poem is very distinct from that fact in conversation. And I
think what really was gained from that sense
of source in common speech was the recognition
that the intimate knowing of a way of speaking
--such as is gained as Olson says with mother's
milk--what's gained in that way offers the
kind of intensity that poetry peculiarly admits.

These words known from one's childhood have
the most intense possibility for the person
writing. Whatever language is removed from that
source goes into an ambivalence that is at times
most awkward. Now a very accomplished man--say,
Duncan--can both attempt and succeed in a rhetorical mode that's apart from this context, although
it may well *not* be; yet Duncan's virtue is that
he can move from one to the other with such
skill and ease. As in "Two Presentations," he
moves to the immediate context of speech (literally, to quotation) yet gathers it into a mode
of rhetoric that is the basic speech pattern
of the whole poem. In other words, it isn't
simply an imitation of common ways of speaking,
it's rather a recognition that the intimate
senses of rhythm and sound will be gained from
what one knows in this way.

Wagner: You have written recently that it is
not the single word choices so much as it is
the sound and rhythm of entire passages that
determines the immediacy of the language. Is

that concept relevant to this discussion?

Creeley: In conversation with Basil Bunting last fall, he said that his own grasp of what poetry might be for him was first gained when he recognized that the sounds occurring in a poem could carry the emotional content of the poem as ably as anything "said." That is, the modifications of sounds--and the modulations-- could carry this emotional content. He said further, that whereas the lyric gives such an incisive and intense singularity, usually, to each word that is used in a longer poem such as his own "The Spoils," there's an accumula- tion that can occur much more gradually so that sounds are built up in sustaining pas- sages and are not, say, given an individual presence but accumulate that presence as a totality. So that one is not aware, let us say, that the word *the* is carrying its parti- cular content, but as that *e* sound or *th* sound accumulates, it begins to exert an emotional effect that is gained not by any insistence on itself as singular word but as accumulation. To quote Pound again, "Prosody consists of the total articulation of the sound in a poem"-- and that's what I'm really talking about.

Wagner: Is line and stanza arrangement still used to indicate what the poet intends, rhythmi- cally? Are poets today more concerned with the sound or with the visual appearance *per se* of their work?

Creeley: For myself, lines and stanzas indicate my rhythmic intention. I don't feel that any poet of my acquaintance whose work I respect is working primarily with the visual appear- ances except for Ian Finlay, and in Finlay's case he is working in a very definite context of language which has to do with the fact that there have been *printed* words for now, say, 400 years. The experience of words as printed has provided a whole possibility of that order as visual as opposed to oral or audible. Ian's working in the context of language as what one sees on signboards, stop signs, titles of books--where the words *are* in that sense; and there is an increasing school of poets who are involved with concrete poetry in that way. But for myself the typographical context of poetry is still simply the issue of how to score--in the musical sense--to indicate how I want the poem to be read.

Wagner: I have noticed in your own readings that you pause after each line, even though many of the lines are very short. You're not just creating quatrains of fairly even shape, then?

Creeley: No, I tend to pause after each line, a slight pause. Those terminal endings give me a way of both syncopating and indicating a rhythmic measure. I think of those lines as something akin to the bar in music--they state the rhythmic modality. They indicate what the base rhythm of the poem is, hopefully, to be.
    The quatrain to me is operating somewhat like the paragraph in prose. It is both a semantic measure and a rhythmic measure. It's the full unit of the latter. I remember Pound in a letter one time saying, "Verse consists of a constant and a variant." The quatrain for me is the constant. The variant then can occur in the line, but the base rhythm also has a constant which the quatrain in its totality indicates. I wanted something stable, and the quatrain offered it to me; as earlier the couplet form had. This, then, allows all the variability of what could be both said and indicated as rhythmic measure.

Wagner: Where in this whole discussion does your often-quoted statement, "Form is never more than an extension of content," fall?

Creeley: Olson had lifted that statement from a

letter I had written him, and I'm very sure
it was my restatement of something that he
had made clear to me. It's not at all a new
idea. I find it in many people, prose writers
as well as poets--Flaubert, for example. I
would now almost amend the statement to say,
"Form is what happens." It's the fact of things
in the world, however they are. So that form
in that way is simply the presence of any thing.

What I was trying then to make clear was
that I felt that form--if removed from that kind
of intimacy--became something static and assumptional. I felt that the way a thing was said
would intimately declare *what* was being said,
and so therefore, form was never more than an
extension of what it was saying. The what of
what was being said gained the how of what was
being said, and the how (the mode) then became
what I called "form." I would again refer the
whole question to Olson's "Projective Verse."
It's the attempt to find the intimate form of
what's being stated as it is being stated.

A few weeks ago I was moved to hear Hans
Morgenthau in the teach-in which was televised
saying, "Facts have their own dynamic." Which
is to say something in one way akin--content
has its own form.

Wagner: Some people use the term "organic" poem
to refer to one in which this principle of
form applies. How does the organic poem differ
from what is usually called the "traditional"
poem?

Creeley: The traditional poem is after all the
historical memory of a way of writing that's
regarded as being significant. And I'm sure
again that all those poems were once otherwise
--as Stendhal feels, Racine *was* modern at the
time Racine was writing those plays. But then
for his work to be respected in the nineteenth
century as being *the* way of writing--this, of
course, was something else again. This is a
respect merely for the thing that has happened,

not because it is still happening but because
it did happen. That I find suspect. If one is
respecting something that continues to happen,
as with Shakespeare, then I agree. But if one
respects a thing that isn't happening anymore,
that is now so removed by its diffusion into
historical perspective, then of course "traditional" becomes a drag indeed. But the traditional is, after all, the cumulative process
of response. It has its uses without question.
But it can only be admitted as the contemporary can respond to it.

Wagner: What of the modern poets who write in
sonnets, quatrains, blank verse? Can they still
be using the organic rationale?

Creeley: Certainly, if these forms can occur.
If they offer possibility of articulation, then
of course they can be used. Valéry, for example,
in *The Art of Poetry* makes some very astute
comments about his own methods of working, and
he found these forms in this "formal" sense to
be very useful to him insofar as they provoked
him to extraordinary excitement and to extraordinary ability. He loved the problem of them.
Now you see, *each according to his nature* again,
to quote from Pound's quote of the Confucian
text. There's no rule. Only when sonnets become
descriptive of values that are questionable,
do I find them offensive. But I don't think
they are *per se* to be written off, except that
they are highly difficult now to use because
society does not offer them a context with
which they are intimate, anymore than society
offers a context for dancing the gavotte.

Wagner: A side issue here, perhaps. Does an
artist's "sincerity" have any influence on the
quality of his work? Can a poet write good poems
about a subject if he has no feeling about it?

Creeley: I don't see how. If one respects Pound's
measure of "Only emotion endures" and "Nothing

counts save the quality of the emotion," then
having no feelings about something seems to
prohibit the possibility of that kind of quality entering. At the same time, there are
many ways of feeling about things; and it
may be that--as in the case of poems by Ted
Berrigan--one is feeling about the fact that
there is no attachment of subjective feeling
to the words. It's a very subtle question.

I remember one time Irving Layton wrote
a very moving poem, "Elegy for Fred Smith."
Later, Gael Turnbull, very impressed by the
poem, said to him, "You must feel very badly
that your friend has died, and your poem concerning this fact is very, very moving." And
Irving then explained that there was no man
named Smith; he simply wanted to write this
kind of poem. But you see, he wanted the
feeling too; he wanted to gain the way one
might feel in confronting such a possibility.
There wasn't, as it happened, a real fact
that provoked this poem, but there was certainly a feeling involved. And it was certainly a "subject" that Irving had "feeling"
about.

This issue of sincerity in itself, however,
can be a kind of refuge of fools. I am sure
that Goldwater was sincere in certain ways,
and I don't think that that necessarily pro-
tects him from a judgment that's hostile to
his intent. But it will gain him a hearing,
as it obviously did. The zealot is often sincere. In other words, sincerity as a quality
is one thing--well, I'd simply point to Louis
Zukofsky's discussion of sincerity in his notes
for the Objectivist issue of *Poetry* in 1931.
But I'm going to take sincerity in my own reference which again goes back to Pound, that ideogram that he notes: man standing by his word.
That kind of sincerity has always been important to me and is another measure of my own
commitment to what I'm doing.

Wagner: No doubt there are pitfalls, too. Eddie

Guest was probably as sincere as anyone writing today. Why wasn't Guest a Williams?

Creeley: Again, you see, we have an easy answer. If we do believe that "Nothing counts save the quality of the emotion," then we have an easy measure for qualifying Guest--the emotion in Guest is of very poor quality. It's so generally articulated and so blurred with assumptional sentiment that it's a kind of mess. It's too general. So that would be the difference between him, I would feel, and someone like Williams who has that virtue of a much more complex and intimate and modulated quality of feeling --and is much more articulate in the area of that feeling, and not only gives evidence of it, but allows its evidence to be felt by the reader.

Wagner: Let's move to a little different issue now, although in a way, I suppose this is still sincerity in a larger sense. Recent happenings have made many of us question what actually is the artist's responsibility to his culture: Lowell's refusal to attend the White House Culture-fest, the Artists' and Writers' Protest against policies in Vietnam--what *should* the artist be doing politically?

Creeley: Well, it's impossible that a man should be only a "fact" in himself. I suppose what Robert Lowell was saying was, among other things, that he simply didn't want to be part of a group of people who were not only admitting but making use of a social occasion that was also a demonstration of commitment to a way of thinking that he himself found very suspect. I know that many of my fellow writers, for example, Allen Ginsberg, Charles Olson, and Robert Duncan in his recent poems (*Passages*) have undertaken a very direct involvement with contemporary political events--as Duncan's poem called "The Multiversity" and the two or three poems that follow it in that cycle show.

These are very abrupt and highly articulate
attacks upon modern political contexts, that
is, literally on Johnson and the administration; also upon the circumstance at the University of California in Berkeley and the
Free Speech Movement.

Wagner: Today's artist should not be an ivory-
tower iconoclast, then?

Creeley: No. It's impossible that a man should
be indifferent to what qualifies him in the
world. That is, my ability to live and make
a living and secure the possibility of family
for myself--this is political. Its *polis* is
the fact of people living together in some
common place and time, as an organization of
people. And all that relates to it is a large
part of life indeed. So that I can no more
avoid political concerns than I can avoid the
fact that it's raining outside.
    Now what I'm going to do about it is a ques-
tion intimate to my own nature and decisions
involved with that nature. I have, for example,
joined in the protest that you mention. And
in my conduct both as a teacher and as a
writer, I would like to think that any time
these concerns confront me I am not only prepared, in some specious sense, but I feel that
there is only the answer that I must say what
I feel--that is, that the Vietnam conflict
called war is an obscene invasion of both
American and Vietnamese life, and that it is
in that sense a moral evil that I cannot support in any sense whatsoever. I will lend whatever time and support I can give to a protest.
But I also remember, because I'm not often
able to involve a political context in my writing, that I felt a kind of dismay that I was
being irresponsible. But then I frankly have
used as a reassurance a statement that Williams
made some time ago (early fifties) on receiv-
ing the National Book Award.
    It goes something like this. "In dreams, as

the poet W. B. Yeats has told us, begin res-
ponsibilities. The government of the words is
our responsibility since it is of all govern-
ments the archetype." And then he notes the
fact that in this conduct of words many poets
have as a result been killed outright or
driven into exile. That is, language is a political act. Anything that enters into the world
as decision of this order involves the political context.

So that I have felt that if in my own conduct as a writer, I could both propose this
kind of commitment I referred to earlier as a
man standing by his word; and if I would not
be blocked or shamed or coerced (as Allen Ginsberg would say) out of my natural skin, that
was possibly my contribution to the political
reality of the time in which I lived. That is,
if I would stand by what I felt to be existent
in the world and demonstrate its reality as
best I could, this possibly gained for me a
political term of responsibility.

I would hate, however, to confuse these
things with what one can call "topicality."
That is, I am dismayed that so soon after the
assassination of President Kennedy there was
a proposal by two men, very sincere and well
meaning in their suggestion--in any case, they
were put to work editing a collection of poems
on the death of President Kennedy. And I questioned that, when I got their letter. I said
first of all, which was probably the real fact,
that I had no poems that were involved directly with his death and therefore couldn't con-
tribute; but further, that I thought they were
making capital so to speak of an event that was
much more profound in its implications than
this kind of use of it would frankly admit. I
felt they were rushing this thing into print
almost too conveniently.

You see, we're back again to Williams' sense
of the government of the words as our responsibility. What outrages the articulation of feeling in language, what makes language subverted

to the meager reality of distorted and finally
criminal acts against men such as are evident
in this circumstance--what distorts and be-
guiles and coerces by means of language can
only, I think, be confronted by a use of language which makes obvious that criminal distortion on the part of those who make use of
it. In other words, it's impossible to either
ignore or to separate oneself from such a circumstance. It means for me personally that
language must be more insistent in its articulations than ever, must be more articulate
in all ways, so as not to lose the possibility
of saying what one feels in a world which has
been given such assumptions that at times it's
a nightmare to think how to confront them with
sufficient energy and definition, to embarrass
them in their own place.

Wagner: In return for this concern, then, should
there be any state or federal responsibility
to the arts?

Creeley: I feel, no. I have never wanted the
patronage personally of any state or federal
government. I feel that it's a very great dan-
ger. Allen Ginsberg, for example, reporting
his conversations with Yevtushenko and the
other poets in Russia recently, said that one
of the largest dilemmas they have concerning
the circumstances of American writers is the
fact that American writers seem to work outside
of the structure of the government they have.
Not that they are indifferent to that structure,
but that they work apart from it. The state in
Russia, Allen was saying and these persons made
evident, is such an admitted fact that it is
impossible for them to think any articulation
can occur apart from its structure. Yevtushenko, for example, had just written a very long
poem, and then was asked by the censors to
make some four hundred corrections. Now he did
that because, for him, it's impossible to think
of how a poem can occur in his situation without

being subject to this limit.

That is, remembering as Olson says, that "limits are what any of us are inside of," for the Russian poet, the state is literally one of those limits which he both respects and accepts. It isn't that he is a "Communist" or anything of that sort so simply, but that he admits this as a real condition of his existence. In order to say anything, he will admit the fact that it must be said in the context of that structure. In this country, you see, we don't have such a total involvement with the government in relation to the people who are living with that government, so we don't have this context. And I would be suspicious of anything that promoted it without full understanding on the part of all involved. I have rather a Thoreau sense of not wanting to belong to any club that I have not chosen to join, which I think is a pretty American insistence.

I have seen, in some sense, what happens when state or federal agencies enter into the context of the university or college. For example, the National Defense Educational Act—scholarships funds and whatever offered to students by the government—has really been a problematic help. It commits the students to saying, as I understand it, that they will never be "Communist," and this, to propose this to someone 18 or 19 or whatever age, is an awfully difficult thing indeed. How do they know that? And then they'll become legally responsible if at any time in their later life they choose this as an identity for themselves. In other words, it's an act which has really created great difficulty. It's a very, very loaded help which, I understand, Eisenhower was critical of, that is, critical of the wording. No, I don't want state or federal responsibility to the arts. I think if they keep the roads paved and provide schools with operating funds, and Medicare, and such things as that, then that is enough for the moment.

In the paper a day ago there was a note
about Johnson's quotation of what he thought
was a poem of Lowell's which turned out to be
a quotation from "Dover Beach" by Matthew
Arnold. In other words, I've never felt that
the distinctions which would be possible to
government persons would be of much interest.
It think that's perhaps why the Library of
Congress, despite its sympathy often to artists,
has never been an active force in the arts;
and why the Poetry Consultant at the Library
has never been an active force during the time
of his occupancy of the chair. Williams' fate
in his appointment, for example, is too often
what happens; and I was interested to hear a
discussion of this last fall in England by
Cleanth Brooks. Both Brooks and Leonie Adams
were Fellows of the Library, and tried very
hard to have Williams reinstated, according to
Brooks, but the point was that the government
agency is apparently much too ponderous, too
intent upon its own structure, ever to admit
the fact that the arts must have a much more
fluid condition in which to function.

Wagner: Without government assistance, what is
the financial answer for today's artists? How
can the poet support himself and his family,
and still have adequate time to write? You
have taught in various colleges; do you feel
that teaching is compatible with writing?

Creeley: I've known so many people with so
many various jobs who were writing that I
don't think there's any one answer. I was listening to a discussion recently in which it
was pointed out that Ives, after all, was a
very wealthy man and that his music is certainly very significant; yet that some other com-
poser micht be poor indeed. In short, the conditions for writing aren't so simply defined.
Each man makes whatever solution is possible.
I've found myself often embarrassed by the fact
that I do have time provided for me, as by

grants; then I'm almost shut up. Simply having
the time designated as time "in which to write"
seems to make that writing impossible. This is
not a plea not to be given such grants, because
I have other uses for them which are very happy; and I feel that the rest and the accumulation of things that they make possible is very
useful to me. But no, I am living as I find I
can, and I assume all other men do the same
thing. Some can't; then it's a question of who
can help, but there's no easy solution.

Poets have been so many kinds of persons
that there is no one solution that will apply
to even three of them. They've been so many
things. As we know of Williams in his own life,
being a doctor obviously was of great importance to him. I don't know what being an insurance executive meant to Wallace Stevens but
it apparently gave him the possibilities he
was after. On the other hand, someone like Lew
Welch, whom I met recently in San Francisco--
the jobs he's done in his life have been important to him: working on fishing boats or as
lookout in national forests. Each man comes to
the solution.

I find for my own case that teaching is compatible with writing; it gives me a way of
living in the world. It earns me the living I
need, and it's an activity that I can respect.
No matter how often I find individual instances
that I don't respect, it gives me an active
voice in something I can respect myself in doing. So that it's compatible with writing in
that it lets me find the world, and it allows
me admission to a world that's constantly coming into being--that is, as I understand it,
as of next year fifty percent of the population
of this country will be 25 years old or younger.
Many of those people are in colleges or universities; that is the context for their activities,
as evidence the Free Speech Movement in Berkeley.
So it's a very interesting place to be now.

Wagner: We hear frequently that this is an

excellent period for poetry, that from all
the present experimentation will come strong
new modes. As a poet, do you feel as if these
are peak years?

Creeley: I don't feel so simply that these
are "peak years." I know I feel that we have
been party to an extraordinary experimentation
and a building on the possibilities offered
by Ezra Pound, William Carlos Williams, and,
earlier, Whitman--I think that this last ten
or fifteen years in American poetry has been
perhaps the most rich of any, or certainly
will prove to be as rich as those in the earlier part of the century. What's now happening is something else again; I find that
there's an extraordinary interest in poetry,
and certainly many, many people writing it--
but I've as yet not seen, except in a few
instances, a clear significance of its effect.
For example, recently in San Francisco at the
Berkeley Poetry Conference, I was very interested in the poems of Ted Berrigan. Now they
come from a mode that has been developed partly by Frank O'Hara, more by John Ashbery, and
perhaps even more significantly by Jackson
Mac Low. In Berrigan's poems, words are returned to an almost primal circumstance, by
a technique that makes use of feedback, that
is, a repetitive relocation of phrasing, where
words are curiously returned to an almost objective state of presence so that *they* speak
rather than someone speaking with them. It is
something that Gertrude Stein had been concerned
with. But these people presently are using it
for a most interesting possibility, and I'm
interested in that sense in what they are doing, very much so. I feel that this is probably one of the most interesting new possibilities in writing to have occurred in some time.
Otherwise, I think that there is the usual
activity, but I don't really find much distinction in it. I do not mean to criticize those
persons now writing, but--this may be simply

an instance of my own age at this point.

I feel that these are peak years, however, in regard to the demand that society now makes upon poetry. That demand has never been more insistent. Therefore, let's say the occasion is certainly here. The time is right, in all possible senses. At the same time, perhaps the very wealth of possibilities is itself a slight confusion to people trying to decide which of many things is that most akin to their own circumstance.

I feel for myself that these are peak years indeed. I have everything I want, for example. I think most poets writing must feel somewhat the same, that there's no reason to sit and grouch about not having something because--my god--there's incredible amount of possibility in all senses. Again, what I did find out in Germany was this, that German poets and prose writers also are very interested in what they call "the American vernacular." That is, we are blessed by having a literary language which makes use of the so-called vernacular as easily as it does the so-called literary. We can use either a highly developed rhetorical mode or else we can use a very commonly situated vernacular. And we have no diminishment of the literary possibility in either case.

Wagner: In Germany, then, that's not so?

Creeley: No, there the language of poetry has been primarily a literary language so that poets like Enzensberger and others have been interested to translate poets as Williams simply that they find in Williams this vernacular in such intensity that they hope by translation to gain its use, in the German context. So that there, you see, the modes are much more limited at present. Also, then, that's even more true in the case of France, where poetic language has really so limited the articulation possible to poetry. I was talking to Claude Gallimard about whether or not there were many French poets

of interest, and the only one he really remarked upon was, unhappily, a young poet whose
name I cannot remember--a Belgian, I think,
significantly enough. He was then about eighteen. But he was the *only* one they really had
come upon. In this country, it's possible to
find at least ten or fifteen persons who are
writing with extraordinary qualification.

Wagner: Would you consider them major poets?
In other words, have these strong new modes
appeared?

Creeley: Yes, they've appeared. Pound has given
so many possibilities just in his work that it
will be a long time indeed before they're exhausted. I feel that Pound will take his place
in the context of literature in the same way
that Chaucer did, in offering the possibility
of iambic pentameter or actually the iamb as
a measure for verse. In other words, setting
a mode in the technical performance of the
craft that stays for all the time subsequent.
Or Spenser, in his modulations or inventions,
would be another figure. Basil Bunting is
right I think when he makes a parallel between
Pound and Spenser as being two great innovators
in the art of poetry, whose work may then be
built upon for years and years. So that I think
that these modes coming, both from such men as
Pound and Williams, and from more contemporary
figures like Charles Olson--that the modes are
evident and that now their particular use is
really up to the qualification of each person
who attempts to make use of them.

Wagner: Perhaps we should continue into the big
questions. Talking about "strong modes," what
in your estimation is a strong, or a good, poem?

Creeley: Well, a good poem . . . I've come in
the past few months at least--whether from fatigue
or from a kind of ultimately necessary conserva-
tism--to feel that there can be at least one

kind of primary measure for the activity of
poetry; and perhaps this statement will seem
oblique, but in any case what has really stuck
in my head through the years as a measure of
literature are the two statements of Pound's
which I mentioned earlier: "Only emotion
endures," and "Nothing counts save the quality
of the emotion." Now these offer to me two
precise terms of measure for what the possibility of a poem can be. I don't feel that
what the poem says in a didactic or a seman-
tic sense--although this fact may be very
important indeed--I don't feel that this is
what a poem is about primarily; I don't
think this is its primary fact. I feel rather
it is that complex of emotion evident by means
of the poem, or by the response offered in
terms of that emotion so experienced, that is
the most signal characteristic that a poem
possesses. So, I feel that the measure of
poetry is that emotion which it offers, and
that, further, the quality of the articulation
of that emotion--how it is felt, the fineness
of its articulation, then--is the further
measure of its reality.

And to that, then, I would add two things.
One, the sense of poetry that's evident in
Williams' introduction to *The Wedge* when he
says, "When a man makes a poem, *makes* it,
mind you," so that it has "an intrinsic movement of its own to verify its authenticity"
--in other words, so that it is not simply a
wish on the part of the writer (or not simply
a communication, saying "I'm telling you this"),
but has within it all that it needs to survive
in its own statement. This, I feel, is a necessary condition for a poem that's active.

For one last sort of sense of measure,
apropos how a poem is, I would take Zukofsky's
point that one enjoys poetry with reference
to the pleasure it offers as sight, sound, and
intellection. These would offer for me three
primary conditions of a poem's activity. And I
would much respect them.

From all of this--I can't answer such a question directly because I don't think it's a case of having an absolute measure that defines an absolute poem. I simply use these senses of poetry in my own approach, in reading. I don't do it at all consciously, but when I have read and have been moved or engaged by a poem, very often I realize that this is the *why* of the circumstance. This is how it has happened.

Wagner: Would your answer be any different had I said a good *contemporary* poem?

Creeley: No, it wouldn't be. I have no interest in *contemporary* as a sense of *the latest*. I remember reading years ago in the work of a linguist, Joshua Whatmough, a very simple book called *Language*, his comment that poetry had said nothing different for the last 6,000 years. And perhaps now that we can go back farther in time, we will find that poetry has not said anything so different in the past 20,000 or 30,000 years. As Olson suggests, its concerns have always been war, the love between man and woman or man and man, friendship. And then the seasons and the insistent change they make manifest. And, finally, the care of the earth, the literal experience of being able to live in a physical place. They have been a curiously insistent set of themes. I don't know, war is the most intense and perhaps the largest political possibility ever experienced by men; and then the most intimate measure of his life is his love for woman or that of woman for man, man for man. So that is is here, at least, contemporaries can relate.
    I would use the word *contemporary* in Stendhal's sense of it. (I might say that Stendhal is probably the one writer whom I've had consistent regard for since I was reading anything at all. I'm just now rereading some of his work, and I'm struck again by the incredible clarity and fluidity of his thinking.) That is, it's necessary

to articulate these kinds of possibilities in
the intimate language of one's own reality.
That is to be modern, he felt. To borrow the
language of other times and places when it is
not intimate is to risk faking--even though
one be very sincere. It is like making old furniture. Even though the piece may be an exact
replica, the situation of the authentic is
always particular. When that aspect of time
and place is removed from it, it becomes a
curiously vacant thing. So I don't think that
I would have spoken differently of a good contemporary poem, because a poem that is active
in these ways that I've tried to suggest is
always active in these ways, if it can be understood at all. Its language may simply be
lost to us by some effect of time or a shift
in the dialect, where we have lost the ability
to read, of course. But, that aside, I would
feel that a poem is continually active and
that time, in the historical sense, is of no
interest in a measure of the poem's activity.

Wagner: Generally speaking, do you think that
the criterion of "meaning" is important to
most modern poets? I was reading the other
day a poem by Gary Snyder, "How to Make Stew
in the Pinacate Desert": " . . . Now put in
the strips of bacon./ In another pan have all
the vegetables cleaned up and peeled and sliced./
Cut the beef shank meat up small . . . ." I'm
going to be argumentative here and ask, if
technique is the rationale for Snyder's poem,
have we gone too far with the emphasis on technique?

Creeley: I was struck by a definition of "meaning" that Olson offered at the Berkeley Conference. He said simply, "That which exists through
itself is what is called meaning." That kind
of meaning, that kind of signification, is what
a poem is. It *does* so exist through itself,
through agency of its own activity; therefore,
is; therefore, has meaning. What a poem says as

some kind of instruction that can be understood and then thrown away--I find this kind
of meaning to be very secondary, to be finally *not* that which qualifies poetry in the
active manner.

About Snyder's poem. The context of the
poem is very relevant; I perhaps know too much
about it. For example, it is addressed to two
friends. What Gary's here doing is literally
giving them a recipe for stew, but--*and*, rather
--his way of speaking is evident. A tone or a
mode or a kind of speech is occurring. Yes,
you can literally take this poem as a recipe
for how to make stew, but in this way of saying something there's also an emotional context, a kind of feeling. That, to my mind, is
the significant part of this poem. It's the
kind of address and the kind of feeling that's
engendered by it; and it's the way the words
go in that way that is to me the most intimate
aspect of this poem as poem.

Now, what can we call it? Technique? Sure,
there's technique in that the poem is articulated and held, in the way the words are placed
in lines. There's a speed offered in the way
the line is going there. But I don't think that
he has gone too far, any more than I felt that
the actual record of drilling that occurs in
Paterson was going too far. It seemed to be
very prosaic, but it gave an extraordinary sense
of how far one did have to dig down to find
what was intimate, vital, and living to one's
own needs. Just as the water was only to be
found after having gone through all those levels,
the very character of that report gave a real
sense of what it is like to try to find something living in an environment that is so
covered, so much the accumulation of refuse,
and waste, and tedium, and misuse. So that I
would rather not in that way talk of "technique"
as something extensible or separate from the
actual circumstance. And I would have respect
for this particular poem of Gary's. Again I
fall back on Pound's "Only emotion endures."

This particular emotion is of an address to
friends meant as a warmth which all three shall
share, therefore anyone. In that possibility
I find the most interest.

Of course I'm interested in how he did it,
but I don't feel that he has gone too far with
technique. It's very simple indeed; it's primarily blank verse, and that's been evident
for many years. One could go to Milton and find
much instruction for writing it.

Wagner: You are one of the few modern poets,
Bob, to escape the charge of "all means and no
matter." Did you--do you--consciously choose
your subjects?

Creeley: Never that I've been aware of. I may
make too much emphasis upon that, but I can't
remember ever setting out to write a poem literally about something that I was conscious of
before I began to write. Again I fall back on
Williams' sense which I may misquote. It's in
the *Autobiography*, where he says in answer to
the very usual charge of his lack of profundity
that dogged him all during the forties and into
the fifties (that was when he was being attacked
for being involved with "nonpoetic" subjects
and for things which were "trivial," etc., etc.,
--again, you see, that's what "meaning" in the
secondary sense can land on someone. It seems
to qualify them as being specious or insignificant. In other words, if the meaning in this
secondary manner is not addressed to something
that seems very ponderous indeed, then the man
writing is charged with being "unprofound." It's
a very, very silly way to think of poems, and
I suppose that what has come to correct that
"meaning" is something partly akin to haiku
where it's very evident that a few words indeed
about extraordinarily common things or sights
or feelings can provoke an endless wave of emotion, as long as it's held in mind). But in any
case, Williams says, "The poet thinks with his
poem. In that lies his thought, and that in

itself is the profundity."

For myself, writing has always been the way of finding what I was feeling about what so engaged me as "subject." That is, I didn't necessarily begin writing a poem about something to discover what I felt about it, but rather I could find the articulation of emotions in the actual writing. I came to realize that which I was feeling in the actual discovery possible to me in the poem. So I don't choose my subjects with any consciousness whatsoever. I think once things have begun--that is, once there are three or four lines, then there begins to be a continuity of possibility that they engender which I probably do follow. And I can recognize, say, looking back at what I have written, that some concerns have been persistent, e.g. the terms of marriage, relations of men and women, senses of isolation, senses of place in the intimate measure. But I have never to my own knowledge begun with any sense of "subject."

In fact, I fall back on that sense of Olson's where--I think it's "Letter 15" in *The Maximus Poems* where it goes: "He sd, 'You go all around the subject.' And I sd, 'I didn't know it was a subject.'" You see, I don't know that poetry has "subjects" except as some sort of categorical reference which persons well distinct from the actual activity put upon poems for, I suppose, listing in library catalogs. Poetry has *themes*, which I feel are somewhat different; that is, persistent contents which occur in poetry willy-nilly with or without the recognition of the writer. These themes are such as I've spoken of, war and the others. But I don't feel that these "subjects" are really the primary evidence of the poem's merit or utility in the society in which it occurs.

Wagner: You don't, then, have any "point" to make, to use a common term of reference?

Creeley: I have a point to make when I begin

writing insofar as I can write; that is, the
point I wish to make is that I am writing.
Writing to me is the primary articulation that's
possible to me. So when I write, that's what
I'm at work with, or that's what I'm trying
to gain, an articulation of what confronts me,
which I can't really realize or anticipate
prior to the writing. I think I said--to ego-
centrically quote myself--in the introduction
to *The Gold Diggers*, well over ten years ago,
that if you say one thing it always will lead
to more than you had thought to say. This has
always been my experience.

Wagner: To look a little more closely at those
themes, then. Many seem to deal with love, hate
--in short, human relationships. Is this human
interaction the dominant interest in your
milieu, from an artistic point of view?

Creeley: Well, I've always been embarrassed
for a so-called larger view. I've been given
to write about that which has the most intimate
presence for me, and I've always felt very,
very edgy those few times when I have tried to
gain a larger view. I've never felt right. I
am given as a man to work with what is most
intimate to me--these senses of relationship
among people. I think, for myself at least,
the world is most evident and most intense in
those relationships. Therefore they are the
materials of which my work is made.

Wagner: Then, in general, are you writing about
what is personally most important to you?

Creeley: Yes. People are the most important
things in the world for me. I don't at all mean
that in a humanistic sense. I am a person. And
how my world is, is intimately related with how
all other worlds of persons can be. So that they
are the most insistent and most demanding and
most complex presence offered to me. I am never,
never apart from that as a concern in working.

Wagner: In some ways, this kind of subject is different from that of many of Williams' poems, which you admittedly admire. Is there a contradiction here?

Creeley: Again, remember what Williams does say, "The poet thinks with his poem." So that when he has a poem such as "The Red Wheelbarrow," which it would be interesting to remember occurs in that sequence *Spring and All*, a mixture of poetry and prose in its original version. That poem, and that whole sequence, is a way of thinking in the world, a way of perceiving--not decided upon but met, that is, almost met in full course, by "divine accident," as Stendhal again says. So that there is a choice; choice does not exist except as recognition. Williams says that that sequence is moving among the recognitions that are given him of the perceptions he can offer. And what I am interested in in those poems is not the --not only, let's say--the literal material evident in the red wheelbarrow, but in how the perception occurs, how he thinks in the context of that relationship. Not simply why does he say this, but *how* he says it, how he gives it credence, how he gives it recognition. I've always been fascinated by this in his poetry --not so much how did he do it as how did he put that car together; to look at or feel or sense or hear, how this way of thinking occurs. I'm fascinated by the way people think and feel (thinking is feeling and feeling is thinking and so on). The materials of Williams' poems in a literal sense are not indifferent to me by any means, since they are the materia of his world, which is very attractive to me-- but I don't feel that it's a contradiction.
  Either he or now as younger men, myself--we are both doing something quite akin: we're thinking, we're gaining an articulation for ourselves in the activity of the poem. As he says, "In our family we stammer until, half mad, we come to speech." That or "the words

made solely of air" that he also mentions in
these two poems from *Pictures from Breughel*.
This context for poetry is one always very intimate and immediately recognizable to myself.
So I don't think that you can say, "Well, this
man talks about green bottles and this man
talks about his wife; therefore, they are not
interested in the same things." I don't think
this is so simply to be said. It's the way
these things are perceived in the poem and how
they are articulated that is significant; and
in that respect I would feel a great debt to
Williams and would feel that I had learned
much from him indeed.

Wagner: What is the modern poet to do, then,
with Eliot's objective correlative? For instance, your poem "The Immoral Proposition"
is successful, but it seems to have nothing
one could relate to this particular term.

Creeley: The catch in that whole preoccupation
is the literality that's intended and, unhappily, it isn't the kind of literalness that
really is consistently useful in Williams' writing. The question is whether or not one will
admit something like "I feel sick" as being a
literal condition or a literal thing, let's
say. Does feeling sick have a literal occasion?
Or is it an abstraction. We'll say you feel
sick because you haven't eaten anything or you
have typhoid or are bored; you know, there are
many contexts in which that statement could have
meaning. So that what I would try to make clear
here is that in a poem like "The Immoral Proposition," I am involved with the substance of an
emotion, with a very distinct content of feel-
ing--which I hope is evident in the poem. A way
of feeling in some circumstance that I feel to
be substantive. I don't obviously claim for it
a like substantiveness as, say, what a block of
wood proposes or a stone, but at the same time
I feel that feeling is substantial and is literal and can be articulated; and I am working my

way through its terms in that poem. Again, in
a sense, I am feeling my way along as I am
writing.

So that if it's abstract, it's abstract in
quite a different way than, say, those statues
of hope. I'm not trying to make emotion *less*
substantial in the poem. I'm trying to articulate it and all that I can feel in it, as I
confront it in the writing. I'm not trying to
summarize it nor to conclude it nor to take
it away from its active environment. I'm really
trying to gain the experience of that environment as I am writing. So again you see, I would
feel the very end of that poem offers the most
succinct statement of what abstraction or this
kind of egocentric possibility in itself does
lead to: "The unsure / egoist is not / good
for himself." That's a real condition. That's
not abstract. I meant literally, that he's not
good for himself in that he tends to be stuck
in self-destroying conjecture: he worries all
that he confronts to pieces because he is so
unsure in his activity, and simply ends by de-
feating the possibilities of his own life.

But, no, *abstract* means removed from its
condition, removed from its own term--to drag
away, literally, as with a tractor. That kind
of abstraction I've always felt a great uneasiness about; but when the situation of some thing,
be it emotion or actual potato, is left to
exist in its own intensity and in its own organization, then I don't feel an abstraction
is involved. And *objective correlative*, by the
way, as a literary term is a very unwieldy and
awkward and very deceptive sense of things, I
feel, because it tends to the context of symbolism. It proposes that the thing for which
there is an objective correlative is in some
way a symbol of that object. And I feel that
that really is the disastrous mistake. There's
nowhere else for things to be except where they
are, and if this is realized, then much time
indeed is saved. Words are things too. If I say
"I love you" or "I hate you," each one of those

words--I-love-you--is a thing. Words are things
just as are all things--word, iron, apples--
and therefore they have the possibility of
their own existence.

Wagner: While we are discussing the subject
matter of your poetry, let me ask about your
most recent book, *The Island*. That's wrong,
isn't it? *The Gold Diggers and Other Stories*
would now be the most recent. Well, using both
the stories and the novel, the prose seems to
me very close to your poetry, not only in its
careful, polished style, but in its themes. Do
you feel that all your work to date is of a
piece?

Creeley: Effectively so, by no means intentionally so, but insofar as any one man is
this kind of thing we've been talking about--
or does have this insistence of his own existence and his own organism and his own organization as such--just so all that issues from
him is particular to himself. I don't mean
style. I mean if it's the issue of him, then
it will have a continuity, whether he intends
it or not.
    I remember years ago, again in a letter from
Louis Zukofsky about one of the books I had
sent him of my own--after talking about the
various poems in it, he said, "Well, we write
one poem all our lives." In other words, any
one part of that poem may or may not have individual significance, but it all goes together
as one continuing writing. To make divisions
in it is a little specious because it does in
that way necessarily cohere. I find, then, that
I can't write outside of my own "givens." These
are the things that I'm given to work with and
I can try to escape them, but I never succeed
in any interesting fashion. So that for me the
novel is the continuing of writing that I've
been trying to do now for almost--what?--twenty
years. It doesn't take a place apart from the
poems, nor is it different from the poems in its

concerns. It's all an attempt to articulate
some complex of feelings that are gained through
the writing, that otherwise are not to be
gained. I remember one time in conversation
with Ramon Sender, he was saying, "Well, anyone, an eleven-year-old schoolboy can write a
poem. The emotional equipment is there even
that early. But," he said, "now think of the
problem of gaining an articulation and an
actual placing for each word in a novel--that's
50,000 to 75,000 to 100,000 words which one is
responsible for, the conduct of each word."

Now a novelist that I respect does feel
that way about what he is doing, and I certainly felt that way about this novel: I felt
that each word had to have as much justifica-
tion in its own position as, say, any word in
a poem. I'm not here claiming that the novel
is a poem because they are very different modes,
but I felt that a novel was responsible to
words in just the same way that a poem is
responsible, and that the conduct of words in
either situation had to be the responsibility
of the writer in all possible senses. Not that
he had to "justify" them by some explanation
specious to their activity, but that they had
to engage in an articulation that was significant to his own feeling. And that they had to
find their place in the context in that way.
Elsewise it was all a proposal of not very
much interest at all.

Wagner: With all this personal feeling in a
work, how can the writer avoid writing a "true
confession" story? The age-old problem, how
does he maintain the proper perspective, whatever that may be?

Creeley: There is no "proper perspective."
Really, I can remember in writing classes in
college, one professor would tell us, avoid all
autobiographical reference because you will have
such a subjective sense of it that you will not
be able to approach it coolly or objectively.

Therefore you'll find yourself involved with
distortions because of your writing about yourself. It will be disastrous, etc., etc. Then
I'd go into another class and be told there
that all one could really use was autobiographical material because that's all one really knew.
All the rest was too removed from the intima-
cies or intensities of one's own experience.
You see now, either of those adamant rules is
a little specious.

One *knows* in writing, I don't know quite
how, but one knows what one needs and one
takes it, without embarrassment and increasingly with a demand that's not to be gainsaid.
So that there's no reason why one shouldn't
write a true confession story. Again I'm thinking of Stendhal who wrote a brilliant true
confession story, *The Life of Henri Brulard*,
and equally something like *Lucien Leuwen*. Or
there's a quote to the effect of Stendhal saying apropos Julien Sorel, "Julien Sorel, c'est
moi." Again, writing makes its own demands,
its own articulations, and is its own activi-
ty--so that to say, "Why, he's simply telling
us the story of his life," the very fact that
he is telling of his life will be a decisive
modification of what that life is. The life
of the story will not so simply be the life
of the man. The modifications occurring in the
writing will be evident and will be significant.

I don't feel that a proper perspective is of
any use except in cases where there is a clear
need for it--that is, to keep your head while
others all about you, etc., etc., à la Kipling.
There are circumstances evidently where that
kind of coolness or objectivity is much required. Or there are kinds of writing in which
it is. But in writing it doesn't really matter
whether one is literally out of one's head with
the insistence of what's being said, with the
emotional demand of it; or whether one is working at a cool and quiet and objective remove
from what the material suggests as emotional
possibility. Again, you see, Rousseau's

Confessions--that to my mind is an extraordinary work. I'll never know Rousseau, any more than anyone else will, but that book is a great relief of feelings that are very much of the human context. Therefore their admission into the writing with such intensity and clarity is already a great relief of all that surrounds him. To read that book is to be relieved.

   In other words, I've never felt that writing was fiction, that it was something made up about something. I've felt that it was direct evidence of the writer's engagement with his own feelings and with the possibilities that words offered him.

Wagner: The issue of "distance," then, is an invalid one?

Creeley: The distance is dictated by the poem, not by the writer. Or the assumptions he may bring to it. The writer may begin writing coolly about something about which he feels no possibility of involvement exists, though why he should want to write about such a thing I don't really know, but suppose he does so begin. To me, it's such a large absurdity; it would be like living with someone from whom one could maintain a discreet distance. What would be the point of that? Writing to me is the most intimate of all acts; why should I want to maintain a distance from that which engages me in it? True, there are times in writing when I want the sight of something, or when I want to gain the view of it that will rid it of my assumptions about it. But that distance, you see, is dictated by something very intimate in the writing. It's not to be proposed prior to the writing unless one is writing instructions for assembling washing machines. But, again, the circumstance will dictate that need much more ably than the writer can propose, and much more significantly.

Wagner: I've been interested in this matter of

the difference between poetry and prose, Bob.
Since you have been writing both for many years
--with the short stories the earlier, of course
--what do you find to be the major differences
between the two modes?

Creeley: Well, let me again speak personally.
The differences as they exist for me are these.
Poetry seems to be written momently--that is,
it occupies a moment of time. There is, curiously, no time in writing a poem. I seem to be
given to work in some intense moment of whatever possibility, and if I manage to gain the
articulation necessary *in* that moment, then
happily there is the poem. Whereas in prose
there's a coming and going. Much more of a
gathering process that's evident in the writing.
In fact I think I began prose because it gave
me a more extended opportunity to think in
something--to think around and about and in
terms of something which was on my mind. It
hardly gave me this sense of objective distance
we've just been talking about, but it gave me
the possibility of stating the thing that occu-
pied me in a variety of ways.

For example, an early story like "Three Fate
Tales" would be an example of this. It's fairly
clear what's on my mind there--how is one in
the world--and these three takes on that sense
of situation are really what the story consists
of. Also, I was involved at the time I wrote
the novel . . . well, I was very interested to
gain the use of something that would go on, that
would give me a kind of day-to-day possibility.
Now in the actual writing I found that it occurred quite otherwise; that is, in some ways
I was back to a circumstance which I had come
to know in poems. And I must note here that
stories were usually written the same way--in
one sitting; so that I wasn't really aware of
how much time they were taking until I'd finished and looked at the clock. Maybe two hours
or four hours had gone by, and I'd been writing.

But those stories too had the same kind of

context, and the same sense of demand in them
that the poems came to have for me. I think
that I was probably more articulate in prose
than in poetry at first, in the early fifties,
as the second issue of *Origin* will probably
show. You can see from that kind of evidence
that prose was much on my mind; I was more at
home with its possibilities at that time than
I was with poetry's. In any case, prose lets
me tinker, rather than work in the adamant
necessity of its demand upon me. I come and
go from it. I can work at many levels of response and can articulate these many levels--
whether intense or quite relaxed or even at
times inattentive. Prose, as Williams says,
can carry a weight of "ill-defined matter."
Well, I don't know if it's necessarily ill-
defined but it can be random, and even at
times indecisive. It doesn't have to say everything, so to speak, in one intense moment.

Wagner: And poetry does.

Creeley: Usually. And also this sense of continuity, of having something there day after
day was something I've had a great longing to
have the use of. I had distinctly envied Olson
the possibility of the *Maximus* poems--that they
could provide, as Olson calls Pound's *Cantos*,
a kind of "walker" for all that one could feel
in writing--or by means of writing. Robert Duncan had had this also I'd felt in poems like
"A Poem Beginning with a Line by Pindar" and
very much in "The Venice Poem," which was the
first poem of his that really seemed to me
major. So I tried to write a novel earlier,
when I was living in France in the early fifties, but there the program of the writing
became so intrusive that the actual possibility of the writing leaked out--I was so intent
upon how do you make a transition from one
chapter to another that this is really all
that survived in the writing. I did get from
one chapter to another with some grace, but

what the actual writing was doing was largely
lax and ineffectual. I don't mean that it had
to move mountains but it was really unengaged
except by the technical concerns that I was
then trying to work through.

Wagner: Any explanation for this state of
affairs?

Creeley: Well, I didn't really have anything
on my mind of much pressure, of much necessity.
Whereas the stories of that same period--"The
Grace" and "The Party"--were much more intensive and much more an issue, I would feel now,
of things I was confronting in my life. Therefore I would feel they are much more pressured.
They have the fact of reality and the pressure
as I would always feel again those two things
to be a necessity. I think that's a quote from
Olson--or from myself. I can't remember which.
    So, talking then about the differences.
Those are some of them. That is, for me personally poetry is an intense instant which is
either gained or lost in the actual writing.
Prose is much more coming and going, though
my own habits in writing prose are very much
like those I do have in writing poetry: I don't
revise as a rule, I find it necessary to begin
at the beginning, to go forward, so to speak.
I remember again in conversation with Sender,
he asked "Why don't you simply begin at some
point that's of intense interest to you, to
what you think to be dealing with?" I said,
"Well, I can't really do it that way. I can
only come to that. I can't anticipate it by
going to it directly. I have to arrive at it,
and I don't even--curiously--know what that
point will be. I'll have to find it." Not at
all to be sentimental, but I think again that
writing for me is a process of discovery, and
I mean that very literally: a way of finding
things, a way of looking for things, a way of
gaining recognition for them as they occur in
the writing.

Prose offers me a more various way of
approaching that kind of experience than does
poetry, but then I do have the sense that
Pound speaks of in *Make It New*, that one chafes
if something in prose is of interest, to have
it, frankly, in the articulation of poetry.
Simply that poetry offers the finer and the
more intense articulation. Now this isn't always true in the sense that there are moments
in prose without question (in the writing of
Stendhal again) which are as intense and as
charged as any I've ever experienced. This is
certainly true of Lawrence, and of Dostoevski,
and of many prose writers indeed who have this
ability to articulate a very intese emotional
context; but the finer articulation is possible
for me in poetry. With one exception, that I
am embarrassed as yet to manage in poems the
kind of coming and going that I've only been
given to manage in prose.

Wagner: Of the two modes, which do you prefer?

Creeley: Well, again, I don't prefer either.
I'm led to use either as I can.

Wagner: A matter of necessity, then?

Creeley: Yes. When poems offer--just that they
come to be written, then I feel very akin to
Williams in that sense he speaks of in "The
Desert Music," apropos the question, "Why do
you write a poem?" "Because it's there to be
written." I've never really to my own knowledge
had any other sense of why things are written.
They simply come with such a presence that one
does or doesn't manage it as one's own abilities can. But--I don't prefer it either in that
way. I don't say poetry is more useful for me
in this sense, and prose in that sense; and
therefore I write a story when I want this
effect, and a poem when I want that effect. They
come and go.

When something's been on my mind for a long,

long time and I've been in some sense conscious
of it, then very often it will be prose that
gives me the possibility of articulating what
is so dogging me with some emotional insistence.
I've been thinking, for example, recently of a
park in England where I was sitting with a
friend, and I was very new; I felt not alien
but freshly arrived, as I was. We were sitting
in this quiet park on a Sunday afternoon, a
small sort of intimate family park with walks,
not hidden exactly but people moved along almost corridors of trees and plants so that one
had a constantly changing vista of persons as
they came and went. And then there was a kind
of old statue, not particularly distinct or
admirable but sort of interesting as a kind of
old person that had suddenly been immobilized
or concretized.

But in any case, that moment, sitting on
that bench, talking in this rather random
fashion and watching the people and seeing
children all ages, is really on my mind. Now,
you see, I don't know what I'm going to do with
it--or rather, I don't know what it's going to
do with me. But that kind of insistence--it's
been in my mind, curiously; it's one of the
most intense things which I seem to have gained
in England. I don't know what it means. I don't
understand it. I don't know why it should be--
of all the kinds of experience that I had there
--that moment suddenly is awfully intense. But
you see at some moment that's probably something that's *coming* to be written. I feel it
now, that it's coming, that I shall work with
it. And when I do work with it, I would feel
it will probably be with prose because it's
such a shifting; it has such a complexity in
it that I'll want to move with it tentatively.
Prose allows me a tentativeness which I much
enjoy at times because it's a need. That is, I
don't want to anticipate the recognition of
what's involved so that prose gives me a way of
feeling my way through things. Whereas poetry
again is more often a kind of absolute seizure,

a demand that doesn't offer variations of this kind.

Wagner: You plan to do more prose, I assume, as well as poetry?

Creeley: Yes, I do plan to do more prose. I must say, though, that as soon as I *plan* to do more prose, I do absolutely nothing. I had planned to do another novel because I really enjoyed very much *The Island*; and so having learned in a sense some of the technical possibilities of such a form--that is, having written it--I gained some insight into what technically was possible in a long prose piece. I wanted not to lose it, so I very quickly committed myself to do another novel, which was unwise of me.

Once I had proposed to do the novel, even gave it a title, and had what I thought was a good occasion (those two years I had spent in Guatemala had given me a crazily chaotic impression of so many things and persons and acts --such a wild variability of people in such a very curiously primal place--that I thought, "This is an ideal thing to work with in prose"). But as soon as I plan to do it, I've all but stopped it. I don't know how I am going to get past that. One day I'll simply sit down and start writing. Until that day comes, talking about it is a little absurd because I simply don't work in that fashion. By planning, by planning to do the novel, and by talking about it with my publisher, accepting a small advance and giving it this title and all, I seem--well, one moment last spring, for example, I really got almost hysterical about this and called the publisher and said, "Look, I want to pay you back that money. I'm sick to death of the whole program of this writing." No, again, you see, Pound is so insistent in the basis of my own critical estimations of my own circumstance. That quote he has from Remy de Gourmont, "Freely to write what one chooses is the sole pleasure

of a writer." That is so true. So that as soon
as it becomes programmed in any way, in the
sense that it isn't momently recognized, it's
a very, very problematic context in which to
try anything.

Wagner: Have you any plans for writing criticism?

Creeley: Criticism for me is occasional writing.
I'd never undertake it as anything more. It's
my own attempt to respond to something that's
moved me, and to give witness to that response
and to that which has provoked it. And to define
the character of my own respect for something
that's evident. At times I feel it's a very
weak act on my part, that I've not really measured to that which has offered me measure, as
with Zukofsky's work, for example. I feel a
great ineptitude confronting it because it's
been such a source for me and when I'm trying
to write a review of it, I'm a little embarrassed to gain an articulation of all that concerns me in it. For example, I've committed
myself to do a review of Robert Duncan's *Roots
and Branches*, in 500 words--that will be like
the ultimate telegram.
    Again, I think of critical writing as primarily a response to the act of some piece of
writing that really has been very, very important to my own perceptions, and very important
in my own recognition. And I tend more and more
to shy from critical writing as a kind of chore
or as a way of reporting. For a time I was involved with writing omnibus reviews of books of
poems, and this very soon got impossible. I
found myself playing a kind of odd game of checkers where I would balance this against that; in
other words, I was imposing upon these books a
falsely comparative standard.

Wagner: Does the pursuit of prose of whatever
kind make you any less a poet?

Creeley: Well, I'm not "pursuing" prose. I'm not after it. And I certainly don't think it . . . I would like to qualify the situation of myself as writer: that the modes are the particular possibility that's evident in the situation of the writing as it's being done. And I think that what I would say, if I had the guts or the lack of embarrassment, that I would say that I would rather be a "writer" than a "poet" or a "novelist." So that then I would use whatever mode was relevant to the things given me to write, as *they* determined it, not me. Ideally, one should be able to make use of any mode that gained the most insistent, fullest range of articulation.

Wagner: The use of any mode betters skills, then, of all?

Creeley: Words are the materials of writing, and all that sharpens one's sense of their possibility is useful. Therefore, either prose or poetry can improve skills in the writing of either. I think, for example, I learned a lot about how to *continue* by writing the novel, and it seems to me true that my poems show what's gained in that novel. "Anger" or "Distance" or "The Dream" or "The Woman"--all of these were written after the novel, and all demonstrate that there's a possibility of going on in the poem that hadn't been there previously. There are only a few poems of this order prior to the novel--one is "The Door," but its sequence is determined by an almost rhetorical term of argument. I had been depending upon a continuity that was taken pretty directly from the rhetorical terms of thesis, antithesis, etc. In other words I followed a habit of organization there that I don't think I was aware of. Much more interesting to me in its organization is a poem like "For Love," but that was curiously a one-time possibility. Since the writing of the novel, when I found how things could drift and shift, and how the line

might encompass that possibility--because the
line is an extraordinarily important part of
the novel's articulation; that is, the way the
sentence is going is very, very important. I
don't mean simply to say that sentence and line
are equivalent but they do offer something of
like possibility in their own circumstances.

Anyhow, I'd learned things from the novel--
how to approach, how to feel things--that were
then useful to me in the poems. And I think
poems like those I mentioned come pretty much
from the experience. I remember Duncan saying
that he felt that the rhythmic articulation
in the novel had really gone beyond what the
poems prior to it had accomplished. And I would
feel him right.

But you see, I'm not interested in being a
poet or a novelist as something that has a
stable content. I don't think that being a
prose writer makes one less of a poet because
I don't think one is made--except in historical
reference--a poet or a prose writer in that
sense. I'm very much against the kinds of division that, for example, led to Lawrence's poetry
being ignored for such a long period when his
novels were so much appreciated. That kind of
division is specious. If a man's a writer, very
often one will find the same intensity of possibility in all that he does. Very often, say,
a prose writer finds it difficult to move into
the organizations of poetry because they are
very, very articulate and if much attention
isn't given them, they don't just fall simply
to hand. It's a highly articulate craft which
is accumulated with many hours and years of
attention, but I find, for example, Pound's
prose is just as interesting in many senses as
is his poetry. The critical writing, not only
in what it says but in the way it's written,
is a very vivid and intense kind of prose. I've
learned from it. I think, again, that some of
Lawrence's poems are magnificent, and the kinds
of intensity they possess are those familiar
to me in his prose also. So I don't like these

kinds of specious division that say a man is
"either-or," and that no actual relation between the two circumstances can easily exist.

Wagner: In speaking of the methods the poet
uses to reach his poem--the forms, rhythms,
other devices--I am always curious about the
actual writing itself. One hears so much about
the conflict between a supporting occupation
and writing. How long does the writing of a
poem take for you?

Creeley: For me, it's literally the time it
takes to type it--because I *do* work in this
fashion of simply sitting down and writing,
usually without any process of revision. So
that if it goes--or, rather, comes--in an opening way, it continues until it closes, and
that's usually when I stop. It's awfully hard
for me to give a sense of actual time because,
as I said earlier, I'm not sure of time in
writing. Maybe to me it seems a moment and it
could have been half an hour or a whole afternoon. And usually poems come in clusters of
three--three to six or seven. More than one at
a time. So that there will be a period in which
I'm writing. I'll come into the room and sit
and begin working simply because I feel like
it. I'll start writing and fooling around, like
they say, and something will start to cohere;
I'll begin following it as it occurs. It may
lead to its own conclusion or to its own entity.
Then, very possibly because of the stimulus of
that, something further will begin to come.
That seems to be the way I do it. I have no
idea how much time it takes to write a poem in
the sense of how much time it takes to accumulate the possibilities of which the poem is the
articulation, however.

Wagner: Your surroundings during the time both
of accumulating and writing--how significant
are they?

Creeley: Milieu--what each person will need
for what he has to do, cannot be qualified
simply. Allen, for example, can write poems
anywhere--trains, planes, in any public place.
He isn't the least self-conscious. In fact, he
seems if anything to be stimulated by people
around him and by moving in large situations
of people. For myself, I need a very kind of
secure quiet; not so much from the noises of
the house--Beatle records in the next room, I
could write with. I usually have some music
playing, just because it gives me something,
a kind of drone that I like, as relaxation.
It helps me. I remember reading that Hart Crane
wrote at times to records because he liked the
stimulus and this pushed him to a kind of openness that he could use. In any case, the necessary environment is that which secures the
artist in the way that lets him be *in* the world
in a most fruitful manner. Some people love
much company; some love very little. I tend to
be a man who feels best in some kind of privacy.
I have very close friends and happily a large
number of them, but I don't find them easily
met or easily gained in large clusters. I don't
like large parties; I don't like to be confined
only to literary people, because I do have a
kind of uneasiness about the "rest of the world"
and therefore I'm much reassured when I have
friendships with men or women who are quite
apart from the literary process or activity.
I like a family. I'm very involved with domesti-
city as a fact or as a condition of living. But
it's hard, again, it's awfully hard to make a
general answer to such a question.

Wagner: What is your concept of the creative
process *per se*? Would you agree with Williams'
description of it? theoretic know-how plus "the
imaginative quota, the unbridled mad-sound basis"?

Creeley: Yes. One can learn a lot both by reading and by what you've accumulated by writing
yourself. And then it's up to--god knows quite

what it is—it's up to these occasions that
come without much announcement and declare
themselves as Williams says, because they're
there to be written. All the understanding
of process in the world to my mind doesn't
ever guarantee their occurrence. And one curiously never does know just when or why or how
or in what guise they will be present. In
other words, the know-how gives one the further possibility of being able to follow what
is so being declared. That takes all the accumulation of technical ability that one can
muster. And it's awfully frustrating to feel
the thing shifting and realize one doesn't
have the competence to follow it. This is a
very unsettling and irritating event. That's
where the technical ability does make a difference.

Wagner: No one can learn to write poetry,
then? This total involvement of the poet—
experiences, knowledge, technique, emotions—
one is a poet perhaps by virtue of what he is,
not by what he knows?

Creeley: He's a poet in the sense that he's
given the possibility of poetry by what seems
to be a very mysterious process indeed. At the
same time, all that he knows from his own writing and that of other writers helps to gain him
as much articulation as he can manage with what
is so given him to write. It's rather like driving. A man who can't drive at all is obviously
embarrassed to go down a road that's opening
before him. The most articulate driver is he
who can follow that road with precisely the
right response to each condition there before
him. I would feel those might be in some way
equivalent contexts.

Wagner: You speak a great deal about the poet's
locale, his place, in your work, particularly
in *The Island*, of course. Is this a geographic
term, or are you thinking of an inner sense of
being?

Creeley: I'm really speaking of my own sense
of place so that I want to avoid "a" sense of
"the" poet's locale. I mean many things. I
mean something like where "the heart finds
rest," as Duncan would say. I mean that place
where one is open, where a sense of defensive-
ness or insecurity and all the other complexes
of response to place can be finally dropped.
Where one feels an intimate association both
with the ground under one's feet and with all
that inhabits the place as condition. Now that's
obviously an idealization--or at least to hope
for such a place may well be an idealization--
but there are some places where one feels this
more intensely possible than others.

I, for example, feel much more comfortable
in a small town. I've always felt so, I think,
because I grew up in one. I like the rhythms
of seasons, and I like the rhythms of a kind
of relation to ground that's evident in, say,
farmers; and I like time's accumulations of
persons. I loved aspects of Spain in that way,
and I frankly have the same sense of where I
now am living. I can look out the window up
into a group of hills seven miles distant from
where the Sandia Cave is located, the oldest
evidence of man's occupation of this hemisphere.
I think it dates back to either 25,000 or
30,000 B.C. and it's still there. And I can
think of this place as a place where men have
been for all of that time.

And again I'm offered here a scale, with
these mountains to our southeast, which we sit
in the foothills of; with the Rio Grande coming
through below us to the west; and then that
wild range of mesa going off to the west further. This is a very basic place to live. The
dimensions it offers to those who live here
are of such size and of such curious eternity
that they embarrass any humanistic assumption
of men as being the totality of all that is
significant in life. They offer a measure of
persons that I find very relieving and much
more securing to my nature than would be, let's

say, the accumulations of men's intentions and
exertions in New York. So, it is both a geographic term and the inner sense of being
that's permitted by that term.

Wagner: Another aspect of locale, I think, is
the association among poets. I realize you
have just finished participating in the Berkeley Poetry Conference, with Allen Ginsberg,
Charles Olson, Philip Whalen, and many others.
Two years ago you took part in a similar ses-
sion at the University of British Columbia.
Evidently, you feel such meetings are useful?

Creeley: Well over thirty people read at the
Berkeley Conference. Olson, Snyder, Duncan and
myself taught seminars. Ed Dorn read and lec-
tured; John Wieners read. It was a large number of people indeed, all primarily from the
context defined by Don Allen's *New American
Poetry*. It was a very exciting company. As to
being useful, I don't know actually what the
public effect is. There was a very large response to this one in Berkeley; a great many
more people came to the readings than was expected. To see, for example, well over a thousand people giving Robert Duncan after his
reading a standing ovation that lasted for at
least ten minutes is to experience the possibility of a response to poetry that I didn't
think I would ever live to witness.
    I was talking also to Allen who had had the
experience in Prague of one hundred thousand
persons turning out for his having been crowned
King of the May, which was not to give him a
personal accolade but rather to regain this
kind of presence among people in a very literal
manner indeed. This festival has very archaic
roots and this figure--that they had made Allen
--was very significant.
    But in any case, personally, I've become a
little weary of public events. I think I need
some privacy for a time, but I'm always stirred
and moved and grateful for the company that

these conferences do involve. Because I do
live in an isolated sense, that is, away from
many of the friends that I have in this way;
and these are the few opportunities that I can
get to be with them.

I do, however, suspect the universities'
appropriation of these conferences. I think
the universities begin to realize that the
arts are enjoying a very insistent public
approval these days. For example, at Buffalo--
I was there also for the Buffalo Arts Festival
--and was to be in a symposium with Randall
Jarrell and an English poet named Hugo Manning.
Just before the actual meeting these two men
couldn't come and so W. D. Snodgrass and Robert
Graves were got as substitutes for them. We
walked into the auditorium where we found ourselves confronting a crowd of well over 2,000
people, who had come to hear a discussion of
"Poetry Today." Equally, the first day of the
Albright-Knox Gallery's opening of their kine-
tic art show, they had over 14,000 people. And
I understand the Metropolitan Museum is widen-
ing its steps in order to permit the crowds
that now come to it. Also, the number of persons visiting museums, primarily in New York
for weekends, is larger than the attendance at
baseball games in the same area.

But I question the universities' trying to
make the arts a *subject*. And I always will question it. I would much rather feel that the university was reflecting a public concern with
the arts rather than some institutional concern
that wants to gain them as materials for its
own activity. Till they realize that the arts
are not to be confined by their assumptions,
there will always be rancor and a feeling of
misuse.

I came away from the University of California,
for example, feeling in one sense misused indeed,
because we were subject to a structure that
was very uncomfortable and did not permit our
free movement within it. Even such simple things
as the fact that we were not given any help

with housing, we were not given any parking
space for our cars, we were told that it would
cost $75 to purchase a parking permit for this
two-week period because there was no other
means offered. In other words, there was a
curious indifference to ourselves as persons,
having the very real problems of our families
with us in several cases. At the same time we
were, curiously, "stars." We were given great
use in this way. The University of California
at the time of my going out planned a publica-
tion of the seminar, which was happily dropped;
and we were recorded endlessly and by people
as far flung as a professor from the Sorbonne.
National Educational TV was there to film on
location and to interview us outside of that.
But I do question the context if the arts are
to be treated only as further subject matter
for universities; if that's what they're after,
they miss the point entirely.

Wagner: At one time, artists clustered in
several cities. Now, however, there are many
"isolatos"--Vassar Miller, Robert Bly, James
Wright, yourself. Why?

Creeley: Unlike painting, for example, which
does require some kind of location (if you
want to see what's going on in painting you
live in Los Angeles or New York, simply because
the galleries and museums in those places are
active reference), but you can send a book to
somebody who lives five million miles away.
Writing doesn't require that you be present.
And after a certain age--I think when one's
young it is extremely important to be in close
contact with people that are stimulating in a
way that you're all going through, trying to
find what's particular to your own possibility
--but by the age of 35 or 40, one is about one's
own work in a more decisive and more determined
fashion. Once that time happens, then it is
not necessary to be so closely in touch with
others. I, for example, like the isolation, or

at least I find it useful to me. At times I
balk against it very much. But I like it in
that it gives me long uninterrupted periods
when I can work, no matter what I may be doing for a living. I find I can pay attention
to what's really confronting me more simply
in this environment than I can in the city
where I'm distracted by both curiosity and
sympathy, by all that's going on around me.
And it isn't so much that it won't be of use
to me, but I mean, I can't--I've got my work
to do just as these other men have their
work to do, and in order to do it, I need
a time and privacy that's particular to myself.

Wagner: Could we return to associations for a
moment? You've mentioned Olson and Duncan and
Ginsberg frequently. I know you are friends,
but what influence has the writing of, say,
Olson, had on your own poetry? Have any poets
really been important in the development of
your art?

Creeley: It's almost impossible to qualify
that sufficiently. Olson was the first reader
I had, the first man both sympathetic and articulate enough to give me a very clear sense of
what the effect of my writing was, in a way
that I could make use of it. His early reading
of my stories particularly was very, very helpful to me. I found him the ideal reader, and
have always found him so. At the same time,
his early senses of how I might make the line
intimate to my own habits of speaking--that is,
the groupings and whatnot that I was obviously
involved with--was of great release to me. I
had been trying to write in the mode of Wallace
Stevens and it just hadn't worked. The period,
the rhythmic period that he was using, just
wasn't intimate to my own ways of feeling and
speaking. And so, much as I respected him, I
couldn't use him at all. Williams came in too
and he had large influence, but it was Olson

curiously enough in the "Projective Verse"
piece (I think I'm right in saying that the
first section of that is taken in part at
least from letters that Olson wrote me, the
part about from the heart to the line, where
he's explaining his sense of the line and the
relation to breath). So he really made clear
to me what the context of writing could be in
a way that no other man had somehow ever quite
managed.

Denise Levertov certainly in those early
years was very important to me. We talked so
much and exchanged so much sense of mutual concern while living in France. She's very important to me; we both share the respect for
Williams and the interest in problems of writing. Paul Blackburn in the same period also.
Robert Duncan is one of the most warm and sympathetic friends I've ever had, which is very
important to me, and again is one of the most
astute and involved readers I've ever had.
And Allen equally, because Allen reassured me
as Williams had that my emotions were not insignificant, that their articulation was really
what I was given to be involved with. Ed Dorn
--many, many men. It's impossible to list them
all.

Wagner: Would you say that the influence of a
poet's contemporaries is as strong as his "an-
cestors," so to speak?

Creeley: Very, very much so. I think as in the
case of a university, very often students teach
each other more actively than they are taught
by their professors. Except that there will
usually be one or two people of the so-called
"ancestor" type that are very important; Pound
is very important in this way. Williams, although
I felt him in a questionable way contemporary
always; Whitman finally comes to have for me
this possibility, although I must confess I'm
beginning to know Whitman in a way that I hadn't
known him previously. Hart Crane had this effect

for me. Then the very precise beauty in Stendhal; for example, the way the thought was so
free to find its own statement--and to only
move as it was feeling some response. Then the
peculiar beauty of, say, Wyatt or Campion.
Shakespeare in this particular period was
very, very moving to me. Coleridge, I used to
love to read Coleridge in the diversity and
the multiplicity of his statement, as I loved
James for very like reasons. Or Jane Austen.
In other words, I don't think one can make an
absolute statement apropos which of these two
possibilities is the more important. It depends.
It depends simply on who the man is and what
his particular nature leads him to.

Wagner: Do you credit any one writer with a
strong influence on your poetry?

Creeley: I think Williams gave me the largest
example. But equally I can't at all ignore,
as I've said, Olson's very insistent influence
upon me at that early time and continuingly.
Nor can I ignore the fact that the first person who introduced me to writing as a craft,
who even spoke of it as a craft, was Ezra
Pound. I think it was my twentieth birthday
that my brother-in-law took me down to Gordon
Cairnie's bookstore in Cambridge and said,
"What would you like? Would you like to get
some books?" "Gosh, yes," and I bought *Make
It New*. That book was a revelation to me insofar as Pound there spoke of writing from the
point of view of what writing itself was engaged with, not what it was "about." Not what
symbolism or structure had led to, but how a
man might address himself to the *act* of writing. And that was the most moving and deepest
understanding I think I've ever gained. So
that Pound was very important to my craft, no
matter how much I may have subsequently embarrassed him by my own work. So many, many people.
    I could equally say Charlie Parker--in his
uses of silence, in his rhythmic structure.

His music was influential at one point. So
that I can't make a hierarchy of persons.

Wagner: There exists at the moment a large
group of young poets writing what have been
called by some, "Creeley poems," short, terse,
poignant. Will these young writers stay imita-
tive?

Creeley: No, they won't. Imitation is a way of
gaining articulation. It is the way one learns,
by having the intimate possibility of some
master like Williams or Pound. Writing poems
in those modes was a great instruction to me
insofar as I began to "feel" what Williams was
doing as well as "understand" it. And so I
found possibility for my own acts.
    I think therefore that this imitative phase
is a natural thing in artists; and I would feel
it should be encouraged. I think that if so-
called writing classes would use this possibility, possibly they would produce a more
interesting group of craftsmen than is now
evident. This is one way to learn, and it's
the way I would respect, coming as I do from
a rural background where learning how to plow
is both watching someone else do it and then
taking the handle of the plow and seeing if
you can imitate, literally, his way of doing
it; therefore, gaining the use of it for yourself. But what you then plow--whether you plow
or not--is your own business. And there are
many ways to do it.

BRENDAN O'REGAN AND TONY
ALLAN: AN INTERVIEW WITH
ROBERT CREELEY

---

*O'Regan and Allan, students from Ireland, inter-
viewed Creeley when he came to the University
of Indiana for a reading in October 1967.*

Interviewer: To start off with something factual:
have you any plans for another novel?

Creeley: I thought to do one apropos of having
lived in Guatemala, with all the variant senses
of person, value and circumstance, but . . .
almost having proposed it, it turned out therefore to stop . . . by which I mean that once it
became an idea or plan, it faded out completely.
Hopefully I'd like to write prose again, but I
don't want to propose anything, because then it
fades.

Interviewer: What exactly made you write *The
Island*? I got the impression that you might have
wanted to cover the ideas of time and change . . .

Creeley: No, because it had been a very large
emotional situation, and, at the time, like they
say, it was one which was resolved by subsequent
living, but still stuck as an emotional center
or crux. Now in another circumstance, so to
speak, it became possible to think of it and to
have experience of it in a way, obviously, that
I hadn't when I was literally in it. I wanted
something that would have emotional density
enough to permit me an occasion not at all of

my own decision that would let me follow it. I
mean it was like a thunderstorm, or something
that was as evident as that and that still was
there. So I thought it would give me an emotional . . . so-called context, or even 'material,'
or an application, in that sense, to start with
and to move with and to see where it goes to.
I thought I knew what I was doing, as do most
people, and I wanted to see what I was literally doing--I mean to experience it, not to ana-
lyze it.

Interviewer: Why didn't you do that in a poem?
Why did you choose the novel?

Creeley: Because in a novel it was easier for
me to move with the variousness of feelings and
circumstances that were involved, whereas in a
poem it's usually some actual concentration or
intensity that's unremitting--that drives to its
own articulation, usually singularly. The emotional circumstances of a poem may be varied
and complex, but the impact tends to be singular. Whereas in the novel--you see you write a
novel, not the whole damn thing at one time,
but you sit down, you write, then you come back
the next day and in the meantime your life has
done this, that or the other thing, but you've
had various experiences though. The novel permits various experience, and a poem tends to be
singular.

Interviewer: To get to poetry, you say that form
is only an extension of content . . .

Creeley: Not *only*, but that form can be previous
occasion of content, no longer actual and no
longer informing. The so-called form that things
have in the world is the particular and peculiar
instance of their own occasion in the world.
Premises or senses of form otherwise seem to me
descriptive rather than what I call loosely ex-
periential and thus actual. If you spill water
on the floor it has a form; now, you can describe

many reasons why it has it--depressions in the
floor, concavity or whatever. Or you can give
things form, you can pour water into a glass,
but the water has form in the glass insofar as
it is water; if you pour other things into the
glass perhaps they won't take that form: ice-
cream for example. So that form is peculiarly
the situation of the content, that is being
form, or gaining form or having form.

Interviewer: Does that mean that when you start
to write a poem, you have a very definite idea
of what the poem is going to say?

Creeley: Not at all. If I knew that I wouldn't
bother to write it. What's the point of doing
what one already knows, other than shoveling
snow or working for a living?

Interviewer: So the poem can explore experience,
then?

Creeley: Right, to have an access to the world
in ways that other kinds of habituation make
awkward. To have information of the world in a
way that moves with formal information, like
knowing how to drive a car, but not being determined by the fact that you do know how to drive
a car only. You see, you can drive to the store
with absolute predetermination to get the bread
and then return home; or you can take a drive,
as they say . . . where the driving permits you
certain information that you can't anticipate.
That to me is much more interesting.

Interviewer: One thing that worries me about
Olson's essay on projective verse is 'objectism.'
I wrote the exact quote down somewhere . . .
"objectism is the getting rid of the lyrical
interference of the individual as ego, of the
'subject' and his soul."

Creeley: Yeah, well particularly now for example
this sense of the lyrical interference of the

ego, of the presupposition . . . You see we're
constantly involved with what we *think* we are,
but the interesting condition is, ultimately,
what we are. There can be a very interesting
correspondence between what we think we are,
and what we thus are evident as being. At this
point, it's interesting to get back to a situation in writing that can be primarily a manifest of what, literally, each particular human
occasion *is*. One sees a poet like Emily Dickinson, who had very habituated senses as to the
context of her own experience, but her poetry
nonetheless manifests a peculiarly evident fact
of not just humanistically being human, but . . .
she says more than she thinks of herself, so to
speak. Now Whitehead, from whom I think Olson
has taken this vocabulary, makes the definition
of human beings as so-called ego-objects in a
field of objects; because humans have peculiarly singular experience of themselves in consciousness. Nonetheless they are still occupying
space and time and have biological fact and so
forth. Olson felt that the assumption of thinking about yourself as being primarily definitive
has somehow been overtaken and even submerged
entirely by the fact of simply being oneself.
The system of human environment had become altogether habituated to the terms of what people
thought it was . . .

*   *   *

Interviewer: How is it that you haven't actually
written a poem about Vietnam?

Creeley: I haven't, unhappily, had occasion to
write one, because . . . It isn't that that
circumstance hasn't involved my feelings deeply,
or hasn't proved in that way a commitment of
them. I'm not ignoring the war as a condition
of human experience or fact, but I'm trying, I
suppose, if anything to say what are the primar-
ies of human existence. The war is a primary
effect on the human condition, but it's not a

primary possibility, obviously, or else I wouldn't
be against the Vietnam war. Gertrude Stein said
a lovely thing about the atomic bomb in 1946 in
an issue of the *Yale Review*. She said if the
atomic bomb is a particular human possibility
then it's awful, no one in his right mind would
consider it to be relevant to the human condition.
It cannot be interesting to human possibility
that you can destroy all life, I mean that's
contradictory. If it's not within the human condition, then it's unthinkable and it's not interesting. So that, on either grounds, the atom bomb
is not interesting. I can't be that glib--she's
not being glib, but I can't put it that simply,
that I don't think the Vietnam war is interesting; but as human possibility I think it's absolutely uninteresting. I don't think that the
murder of people in that fashion, or that commitment of human life is interesting, so I will
not . . . not so much not speak of it, but I
want to speak of what is most deeply *possible*
in my life, even when it's painful.

Interviewer: Couldn't you perhaps write about
the bomb, to go back to that, as a fact of existence, like Gregory Corso?

Creeley: Gregory Corso did, but Gregory was fascinated by the almost bizarre or wildly exotic
imagination that can include the bomb in human
reference. On the one hand one has people talking about the bomb as deterrent or prevention
of this and that, and Gregory wasn't trying to
humanize the bomb, but he was simply trying to
say, O.K., that's how they're thinking of it,
but how else can you think of the bomb? He wasn't
trying to humanize it. I mean, the bomb *is* human,
rabbits didn't make it, or monkeys. It is a peculiar image, an actual artifact, of the human environment, and it's a very weird thing to have
come up with, after all these years.

Interviewer: What about the fact that there's
worse to come?

Creeley: That's *future*, as Olson would say, and
I don't know.

Interviewer: But at least the bomb means death,
but gas control allows people to go on living
without control over themselves.

Creeley: Williams has a lovely line in a poem
that ends "What do they think they will accom-
plish with their ships that death has not already given them. Their ships should be directed
inward. But I am an old man. I have had enough.
The female principle of the world is my appeal
in the extremity to which I have come." It's
not only the bomb, it's all senses of extension,
as though there were anywhere else to live,
except where you literally are. In this curious
biological time-machine that you inhabit, you're
not going to get out of your skin, you know.
Maybe; Norbert Wiener is hopeful that possibly
we can reconstitute our chemical . . . bit.

Interviewer: This is what I meant; this kind of
control is becoming possible.

Creeley: That would involve being humanoid, a
new experience of the world.

Interviewer: How do you think it would affect
the authenticity of the life that exists?

Creeley: I don't know. I think that friends who
are biologists or physicists or computer experts
. . . I was talking to one, working at Bell Labs
trying to reduplicate the context or the fact
of the human voice, trying to computerize it,
so that a computer can speak, with the same possibility as humans. It's not thus far even conceivably possible. We're highly sophisticated
organisms; it may be that there is one aspect
of life that cannot to my mind ever be anticipated, and that is the so-called purposive. I
mean even the most sophisticated intelligences
of our time, I should say, are premising all

their activities on so-called *chance* factors,
or on whatever provides the possibility of chance
environment. Not trying to gain information
from, but trying constantly to situate something
in 'random,' in evidently or experientially random occasion. Because once you enter purpose,
you're stuck with that kind of circumstance that
Heisenberg implies, that observation impedes
function. Once you're going to do something,
you have an invariably different experience of
it than if you were not going to do it, or if
you had not even thought of it. I have friends,
for example, who've meant to have children, I
mean really decisively wanted to have children,
and have therefore set about the possibility of
having them. But life occurs at a moment that
they can never quite experience. When human
beings have become sufficiently sophisticated
or articulate in their proposals for really
realizing life, reifying it, then that will
shift the experience of life into some dimension
that I find almost unthinkable.

Interviewer: You're talking about possibilities
of control here?

Creeley: Yeah. To me life is interesting insofar
as it lacks intentional 'control,' and finds a
situation of its own making. Those of you who
have had LSD, for example, had the extraordinary
experience of finding that you were not separate
from quote life unquote, not in some idealistic
"Gee, I love everybody" way, but you may have
had the experience, as I frankly did, that there
were force-fields, that your toe didn't end
'here.' It wasn't that your toe extended through
time and space to all possible places, but rather that where this toe apparently stopped there
was a force-field that was entering it, that
you were constituted like an oil-slick or a
swarm of bees, that you were not divisible from
all else that was evident in your consciousness.

Interviewer: How do you regard the reality of
that perception?

Creeley: I believe in it, yeah. You see, once
you divide yourself from that situation of experience . . . You see, this is an experience
which seems to be evident not only in mystic
writings; but all that seem to experience life
as occasion seem to feel intuitively or vision-
arily or inevitably this sense of oneness, that
the condition is one and that there is never
more, or less--that all *is*. I mean, think of
the whole vocabulary. I don't think it's coinci-
dental that the vocabulary is so extensive in
time. Either there is some chemical situation
that I'm naive enough not to know about, or
else it's something that's peculiarly the case;
that what we experience--place, time, condition,
organism--is not divisible, that nothing is
more nor less in the world, and that it all is
in some way literally related. We are forms
particular and separate in terms of apparent
containment, but . . . we die, we molder and
that kind of image, we are not separate in some
decisive sense from all other life-forms. The
situation then is that insofar as the ego becomes decisive, the ego has to experience itself as distinct consciousness, as division
from that other experience. You know, the business that Olson at times speaks of with some
bitterness, of "the universe of discourse" where
thought becomes thought about thought as opposed
to the act of thinking, which is not divided
from the totality. So that objectism is to realize that each is in the world as each is, and
is not more nor less than that, not in some
humbler or self-depreciating sense. I mean, you
can go down to the beach and pick up a particular grain of sand and say that this is the 'most'
grain of sand on the beach.

Interviewer: Did you do much reading in Buddhism
or Japanese literature?

Creeley: I've had a lot drummed into me by various friends. I did a course once in New Mexico.
I've been fascinated by Japanese writing, the

haiku, and by people like Blyth in *Zen and En-*
glish Literature.

Interviewer: How would you explain the sudden
flow of values in opposite directions, from
East to West and West to East?

Creeley: Again, ego-structures. Ego-structures
with alternating specifics. The water freezes
or boils,--again condition and experience of
condition, which the consciousness permits to
stay in the world as though it were *the* condition.

Interviewer: Do you believe in a conservation
of this total energy?

Creeley: I don't see how anything could leave
the world. I don't know where it would go. You
get conservation of energy, or you get transformation. I do like that sense of Zukofsky's
"Raise the great hem of the extended world,
which nothing can leave." All that is in it is
in it forever.

Interviewer: But are you not extending from the
real to the imaginary there?

Creeley: I don't know which world is which, really.

                    *   *   *

Interviewer: What do you think the importance of
literary tradition is?

Creeley: I think that literary tradition is most
interesting as the experience of the effects . . .
of something happening and having happened in
the world. I think that literary tradition would
be akin to the evolution of an automobile. It
would be absurd to my mind, if you're interested
in a so-called vehicle that you could make move
by some power-source that it could carry with
it, not to acquaint yourself with previous

information of that same order. You could start
from scratch, and there are many people in the
world who could, who have never seen or heard
of an automobile and could begin from that condition to imagine one. But having grown up in
the United States with all the information of
automobiles--that's tradition to me.

Interviewer: It's like Borges' image of the
man going into the temple. Do you think it's
the same?

Creeley: Taking tradition more as evidence of
something than it really is . . . I mean you're
born in a house and you grow up in it. The tradition of the house is what is evident in your
experience of it, that's what the tradition of
the house is for you, the furniture, or the way
the house sits, or how the rooms are.

Interviewer: And you can get out of the house
if you don't like it?

Creeley: Yeah, you can break with tradition,
as they say, you can go into some other tradition. But it's impossible that human beings,
having been on the Earth in a certain state
for a certain number of years, shouldn't have
experienced, not only as individuals but as a
societal continuity, an inevitable amount of
feedback, which is tradition. That's why I think
that tradition is what can simply be regarded
as feedback from some particular process. The
word's interesting, by the way: 'tradition'
comes from a root that means what one group
surrenders to another.

Interviewer: Are there any English poets that
you enjoy, or that interest you at the moment?

Creeley: Yeah--Basil Bunting most decisively.
Tom Pickard, a favorite of Bunting's, I think
the most articulate younger writer. Again, not
as a break in tradition, because he recalls a

tradition previous to that which has been most
evident. Now Charles Tomlinson would also be
continuing the possibilities of the reform-
ing of a tradition. It's interesting to see in
Tomlinson's writing what ideas come of his interest in, and experiments with, American modes,
because they do become particularly English in
his writing. Anyway, I'm interested in him. A
Scots writer, Ian Hamilton Finlay--I'm very
impressed by his earlier work, and then when
he shifts to concrete poetry entirely, I'm continuingly interested in him. People like Tom
Raworth . . . and then I love the group that
have been primarily from Liverpool, like Adrian
Henri and the editor of *Underdog*, Brian Patton.
Pete Brown I like, and Spike Hawkins. I read in
various places in England in 1964. I talked to
writers like Pete Brown about the problems of
taking on an idiom particular to an environment.
I think that Pete, coming from Liverpool, had
a particular occasion for it. The kind of street
talk, street song--I don't think it's just sentimental that so much of that impulse comes
from there. I think it's peculiarly Irish, and
Liverpool's still a kind of immigrant society,
that has a distinction otherwise than being
Scottish or Welsh or Cornish or Northumbrian.
Being Liverpool, it's something very different
from the other English environment. I've talked
to pure Englishmen, who are very different people.
Some of them I've found extraordinary--I mean I
know people like George MacBeth, and Edward
Lucie-Smith, whom particularly I have a fondness
for; but I think that something went dead. I
think that Denise Levertov and her shift show
what the dilemma of English poetry was for many
people involved.

LEWIS MACADAMS
AND ROBERT CREELEY

---

*The first try at this interview was a failure.
Creeley was ready, but I had just driven the
New York Thruway from New York to Buffalo; and
by the time I got to Eden I didn't have any
questions left to ask. The "interview" ended in
the dark, everybody morose and slightly drunk.
So we adjourned to his driveway to shovel snow.
We tried again two weeks later, in March of 1967.
The snow had stopped, the sun was out, and the
Creeley household was full of friends, the
poets Allen Ginsberg, Robert Duncan, and Robin
Blaser; his wife Bobbie and their daughters,
Kirsten, Sarah, and Kate. After breakfast Creeley
and I went upstairs to his study, a big sunny
room looking out across a long wooded valley to
Lake Erie. The study had once been a nursery,
and the framed photographs of Charles Olson and
John Wieners, and Bobbie were set off by a pink
wallpaper covered with tiny horses and maids.
On one of his bookshelves was a tiny piece of
sculpture by John Chamberlain. The tape continues to roll . . . L.M.*

MacAdams: Why is it in your works that New
England rarely figures as a geographical place
at all? It seems more like a language.

Creeley: As a kid, I used to be fascinated by
people who, like they say, "traveled light."
Perhaps this is the same kind of metaphor that
the *things* my father left in the house after

his death were too--I was very young and these
things were really "my father," whom I never
literally could remember very clearly otherwise. My mother even took care of them, or
kept them, like his bag for example, or his
surgical instruments, or his prescription pads,
or, even to quite a late time his doctor's
bag still had the various pills and what not
in it. It used to be fascinating to take all
these pills and see what they would do to you.
The things were not only relics of his person;
but, what was interesting to me, there was
this instrumentation peculiarly contained in
this thing that he could carry in his hand.
The doctor's "bag," for example. I was thinking of the idiom now, "bag," to be in this or
that "bag." That that doctor's bag was an absolutely explicit instance of something you
carry with you and do your work in. As a kid,
growing up effectually without a father, I
was always interested in the particular people
who entered our house as men, that I had particular feeling for as men, would be men who'd
come to do something; like say, a carpenter.
Or who came with specific instrumentation;
e.g. tools. And what fascinated me as a kid
was the idea that you could travel in the world
--Johnny Appleseed, for example. Or images or
senses of traveling in the world with what you
needed in your own hands. That fascinated me.
And that does come back, for example, when I
find myself talking to people apropos writing.
One of the persistent scenes will be that it's
first of all say, "What a great thing. To be
a writer." That words, you can carry in your
head and they're free. You don't need any particular materials other than the most minimal.
And that given anything, possibly, to write
on; and even if you don't have something to
write on, you can possibly induce your memory
to retain it. That you can really "travel light."
I had minimal involvement with the Depression,
unlike Bobbie, but the sense of being able to
travel with what you need was very fascinating

to me. First of all, people would always be
telling you you ought to carry in your head
what you need to know. And that secondly, you
ought to be able to move at a moment's notice;
because the world was such that if you couldn't
thus move, if you were hindered or impeded by
some necessity to be where you were as though
you could not move from it, that you'd miss
the chance.

MacAdams: How old were you when you left Harvard to go into the American Field Service?

Creeley: Eighteen.

MacAdams: Did you just do one year at Harvard?

Creeley: They did accelerated programs during
the war years, and I entered in the summer of
1943, and so when I left I believe I was in
the middle of my sophomore year. I took a year
off, effectually. And I was a copy boy, living
in Cambridge, but working in Boston. But I was
only that for three or four months. Then, I
was suspended from Harvard. I carried a door
out of Lowell House that the painters had removed to paint. An afternoon. So . . . Then
I remember that was extraordinary, to get on
a boat in Baltimore, and to get off the boat
in Bombay, that was about 28 days at sea, and
sailing through the Mediterranean so you could
see Port Said, for example, but you couldn't
get off the ship because of security.

MacAdams: Did it feel like total dislocation,
or like great adventure?

Creeley: Great adventure. It was fascinating.
It was a lovely time. I was sort of glad to
get out of there. The whole scene around Cambridge was rapidly deteriorating. My job was
getting incredibly tedious. The rapport with
my first wife to be. We were in love, but she
had gone to Black Mountain, and then she decided

she didn't love me anymore, etc., etc., so that was all a very bleak occasion. And this really jumped me into something I had absolutely no anticipation of whatsoever. It was terrific. Grotesquely, thinking of the occasion. But it was terrific.

MacAdams: Had you been in correspondence with Williams and Pound before that?

Creeley: No, no. That only came after I was out of college. We first went to Provincetown where we spent a year. We came to be there because I'd met a man who was very good to me, in the sense that he talked to me a lot, and he was outside the academic scene. He was a writer named Slater Brown. He was at that time at a kind of bleak period of his own life. He was working as a gardener in Belmont.

MacAdams: He's Cummings' friend, "B," in *The Enormous Room*, isn't he?

Creeley: Yes. He was a writer of the same period as Cummings. And I gather he was active on *The New Republic* for a time. And that he was also active on *Broom*. So he thus had acquaintance with Allen Tate and Malcolm Cowley, and he knew all that particular group of people. But his closest friend of that group would be Hart Crane. Slater and his wife were really about the only people of this relationship that Crane speaks of consistently with affection. When I first met Brown his own scene was pretty bleak. He'd been drinking heavily for a number of years. He was effectually an alcoholic. But he had these fascinating stories. And so we went down to Provincetown, which was a bohemian community, and we stayed there for a year. And then we decided, hopefully, to buy a house in New Hampshire. We had a friend who had a place he was interested to sell, which we began to buy. So we lived in New Hampshire for three years near Franconia Notch. It was during this time that

I started writing to Pound and Williams apropos
a magazine I was involved in. That's how I got
up my courage to write them. I would have been
shy of writing them just to say, "I think you're
a great man," or something. You know, I wanted
to have business that gave me reason. And that
happily did. Pound wrote specifically, but he
tended to write injunctions--"You do this. You
do that. Read this. Read that."

MacAdams: Did you do everything he said?

Creeley: I tried to. I couldn't do it all. He
would send books at times which would be useful. *The History of Money* by Del Mar, which I
read, thought about, and so on. He was very
helpful. It was very flattering, to be taken
at all seriously by him. Williams was always
much more specific. And at times would do
things which would--not dismay me--but my own
ego would be set back. I remember one time I
wrote him a very stern letter--some description about something I was going to do, or
this was the way things were blah blah. And he
returned me the sheets of the letter and he
had marked on the margin of particular sections,
"Fine. Your style is tightening." But I had
the sense to know that it was of more use to
me than whether or not he approved of my answers. He would do things like that which were
very good. While Pound would say, "Would you
please tell me how old you are? You refer to
having been involved in something for forty
years. Are you 23, or 63?"

MacAdams: Who was the person to first hear
Olson?

Creeley: Well, Olson had met Duncan when he had
been out on the West Coast. I think in the late
forties. He had been out there, and he had been
introduced to Duncan, and he had had a very
vivid impression of him. He said he went to a
party, I guess, at Robert's place. And he found

Robert sitting on a kind of velvet throne, looking like Hermes himself, or something. He was
very amused and impressed by the incredible
drama that Robert was able to make of the scene.
And "Against Wisdom As Such" would be some of
that. But I think Robert was so involved in his
own scene then, or so involved with the center
of writing he'd got to, that I don't think he
had much interest in Olson at this point. Olson
really comes into Robert's purview, so to speak,
through *Origin*. But the first person, curiously,
to give us access to Olson was Vincent Ferrini.
He heard from Cid Corman that I was trying to
get material for a magazine, and so Cid had
asked Vincent to send some stuff, and then Vincent undertook to send some of Olson's. And my
first reaction was that I wrote back saying,
"You're looking for a language." And, boy, did
he ever come back on me!

MacAdams: What did he say?

Creeley: He said, "Let's take that up. Am I looking for a language?" You know, "Am I looking for
a language? In ways perhaps that you haven't considered." No, I didn't even know how old he was,
frankly.

MacAdams: Were you in New York at this point?

Creeley: No, no. Still in New Hampshire. Then
about a year later, it must have been, we moved
to France. So that I really was writing to him
for almost five years previous to meeting him.
It was a very intensive correspondence, by which
I mean sometimes four or five letters a week
would be going back and forth.

MacAdams: Were you raising pigeons at this point
in the country?

Creeley: We were in the process of buying this
farm. As a kid I'd had poultry, and pigeons and
chickens and what not. We had no ambitions that

this would make us any income. We had a small
garden that gave us produce for canning. And
then the chickens did afford us eggs and meat,
but they were never any real commercial scene.
And we were living on a pretty small income,
and it gave me something to do. It made the
form of a day very active and interesting. I
mean, something continuing: feed them, pluck
them, take care of them in various ways. And I
had met a lovely man, indeed, named Ira Grant,
who was a house painter in Hanover. And he was
also a crazy, decisive breeder of Barred Rocks.
He was a lovely man. Quite small, almost elfin
in various ways with this crazy, intense, and
beautifully articulate imagination. He could
douse for example, and all manner of crazy,
actually mystical businesses that he took as
comfortably as you'd take an axe in hand. No
dismay, or confusion at all. This happened
several times with neighbors in New Hampshire,
e.g. losing money in the woods. You'd just cut
a birch wand, and find it. The same way you
turn on the lights to see what you're doing. It
can be variously hazel or birch, or hard wood,
preferably, that grows near water. You can usually
get it in the form of a forked stick, and when
it dips, there you are. Continuingly, in parts
of New Hampshire, if you wanted to find water,
the most economical and simple manner of finding
it would be to get somebody in the neighborhood
that had this ability, and ask them to come over
and check out various places for you. And they
had good luck. I mean Ira would be almost always
right. I remember one of these neighbors of ours,
Howard Ainsworth, a woodcutter, was cutting
pulp in the woods on a snowy day like. But he
had a hole in his pocket, and by the time he
had discovered it, it was late in the day, and
he'd lost a pocketful of change. So Howard simply cut himself a birch stick and he found it.
It was nearly total darkness in the woods and
he found it. He only remarked upon it, that is,
how he'd found it, as an explanation of how he'd
found it. I mean, it never occurred to him that

it was more extraordinary than that. "Wouldn't
anybody," you know.

MacAdams: How did it strike you?

Creeley: I was fascinated by it. Because it was
the kind of quote mysticism unquote that I could
enter into, because it was so extraordinarily
practical and unremoved from its actual location.
Ira had this crazy way of exemplifying what he
knew as experience of things. He used to paint
for example, you know paint pictures. He showed
me once this picture of a dog. He said, "What
do you think of this? It's one of my favorite
dogs." He showed me this picture of a dog that
looks--it's a picture about this large--not very
big. And it's this white and black dog that
stands there looking incredibly sick. And I
said, "Gee, Ira, it's a nice picture. But."
And he said, "Yes, it died three days later."
He said, "That's why it looks so sick." But he
delighted me, you know; and I felt much more
at home with him than with the more--not sophis-
ticated--because I don't think any man was more
sophisticated in particular senses than he. But,
God, he talked about things you could actually
put your hand on. He would characterize patience,
or how to pay attention to something, or, you
know, how to have not so much continued occasion
as though one wanted it; but how to pay attention
to what's happening. So in a funny way he probably gave me more sense of things than almost
any man I can think of. I have some of his letters still. He wrote in a lovely old-fashioned
hand. A very warm man. Extremely good to us. I
think he sensed that we as a young couple were
really having a bad time, very confused with
ourselves, and very unable to admit our own
condition. And he curiously managed to permit
us to do that.

MacAdams: You were open to it?

Creeley: I sure was. I was very anxious to, not

so much to know what was wrong, but to know
what was this continuous state of frustration.
He never really told me, but he permitted me
to see it.

MacAdams: How come you went to Mallorca?

Creeley: The situation with the house we were
trying to buy was getting very tight. In other
words we fell through on one payment, as it
happened. And the owner decided that since we'd
failed to pay this particular business, we should
either pay it or get out. So we decided that we
couldn't really keep this scene together. It
was just too expensive. The house was awful. It
was a lovely house but it was in complete dis-
repair. We spent an awful lot of money, such
as we had, trying to get it back into shape. I
mean the roof was gone, the floors were gone,
the sills were gone, the whole place was over-
grown with brush that we had to clear. There
were many things that needed repair. We put in
a heating plant. But he got very--I don't know
--I think he just decided it was interesting to
have his house back. I don't think it was some
kind of great economic scene, but I think he
now became interested in the place. Simply that
we had sort of broken the ice. So we were trying to live on, it was literally $215 a month.
So we decided that living on that amount of
money in New Hampshire was really bleak. People
were getting sick. Everything was very expensive, or at least it was more expensive than
that amount of money could provide for. Mitch
and Denise Goodman had gone to France, and we
wrote and asked them what kind of a life was
possible on that income, and they said, "Fine,
you can probably live very well." So we went
over and we ended in a house. Whoo, awful house
we had, although I got to love it. But it had
no lights, no water, no heat, no electricity,
no toilet, no nothing. It had a little wood
stove--this business of crawling around in the
winter out in the woods adjacent to this little

block of houses that sat out in the farm country away from everything, trying to knock down
dead trees and cut 'em up with a marine knife
to burn in the stove. It was really weird.

MacAdams: Do you think you work better in that
kind of isolated position?

Creeley: My habit seems to be so still, although
having been now a teacher for some years I can
make it with a number of people and find a place
with a number of people. But my dilemma, so to
speak, as a younger man, was that I always came
on too strong to people casually met. I remember one time, well, several times this has been
known to me, I tended to go for broke with particular people. Once I found access to someone
I really was attracted to--not only sexually,
but in the way they were--I just wanted to--I
found myself absorbing their way of speaking.
I just wanted to get in them, literally, to be,
to be utterly with them. And some people, understandably, would feel this was pretty damned
exhausting to have someone thus hanging, you
know, like coming at you. And also, I didn't
have any experience of how it was really affect-
ing the other person. I mean, I think that a
lot of my first wife's understandable bitterness
about our relationship was the intensity that
she was having to deal with. I mean everything
was so intense and thus was involved always
with tension, and that my way to experience
emotion was to tighten it up as much as possible,
and not even wittingly. Just "naturally." One
time I remember, I was with someone, Dan Rice,
who's an old friend from Black Mountain, and he
and I were in some situation with other people
and we were talking with someone we'd just met,
and I remember when the other person either had
gone to the john or something, Dan just sort of
said, "Look," you know, "like, don't come on so
strong. It isn't that you're arguing or anything,
but the intensity with which you're forcing this
person to react or to admit you is really getting

a little scary to them." See, I was always trying to push the particular circumstance to where
it would break open, and be quote itself unquote
or manifest itself; and understandably there are,
I mean people in usual, like they say, casual
daily activity don't really like to get, as they
say, that involved. And I found my whole appetite
was to be as involved as possible.

MacAdams: With everybody or just--

Creeley: Literally anyone met I wanted immediately to get into that condition. There are many
kinds of explanation one could think of, psycho-
logically and otherwise. You know a kid growing
up with a peculiarly absent emotional condition
except that there was a woman named Theresa Tur-
ner who continued to live with us after my father's death. She'd been almost literally rescued
by him from a state home for the mentally retar-
ded. She'd come to this country from Ireland as
a young woman about 18 or so to join her older
sister; and on entering the country she was
given some kind of qualifying business that was
customary and the immigration officials decided
that she was not of a mental level that would
permit her to--so they referred her to this home
for some reason and he'd found her there, and
he was a doctor, consulting doctor for this
house in Massachusetts. And he thus got her out
of there and she thus became a member of our
family and worked as a maid or whatever. She
was so devoted to him that when he died she continued to stay with us as a, effectually a housekeeper. But she was really the emotional center
of my life as a kid. Until she died when I was
in my twenties after I'd married. By then she
had left our household and was living again with
her sister and her sister's family. But other
than her--I don't know how many people one needs
--but her inarticulation was very attractive to
me at times--at times it frustrated me awfully
when I was in my early teens. The fact that
Theresa couldn't "get" some things that I could,

say, was very, very frustrating to me. But she
really gave me an emotional response, that my
mother gave me too, but in a much quieter more
unintentionally reserved manner. And she was
also committed to making a living for us so
that she was distracted. But anyhow . . . No,
I loved to get with people, but I didn't have
any sense as to how you do it. I mean I was
curiously lost. My father being dead, I didn't
know what the forms were. How did you be a man?
You know, immediately I thought, "Gee, am I
really going to be, not stuck with, but is it
my life to sit with the girls?" And I thought,
"Well, I certainly feel at home with the girls.
And I dig their emotional condition because
it's been my life." Growing up with five women
in the house, man, I knew all the signs and
gestures and contents, or at least I knew a
lot of them that were manifest in women's conduct. Ways of saying things, ways of reacting,
making the world daily. But I didn't have a
clue as to what men did, except literally I
was a man. It's like growing up in the forest
attended by wolves or something. It took me a
curiously long time to come into man's estate.
The sexual initiation curiously doesn't resolve
what people at times think it does. I mean, they
assume that when you've had sexual experience
somehow you are matured by it. I don't feel
that's true, necessarily, at all. Anymore than
initial sexual experience at the age of 10 or
11, I mean your first experience of your body
as this bag, that this necessarily has with it,
that now today you are a man. So that for me to
get to be a man was extremely awkward at times,
and I learned it from my contemporaries and
from one or two older men who somehow sensed
my dilemma and were able to make forms that
would give me articulation or show me how articulation might be possible.

So anyhow, I came on too strong, apropos
living in isolation. See, I grew up in the woods.
I grew up on a farm in West Acton, Massachusetts,
that was not being used as a farm. My father bough

it prior to his death and it was to be a kind
of place for us to live while he kept his practice or business in Boston, or Watertown, Massachusetts. I could go out into those woods and
feel completely open. I mean, all the kinds of
dilemma that I would feel sometimes would be
resolved by going out into the woods, and equally that immanence, that spill of life all around,
like the spring in New England where you get
that crazy water, the trickles of water every
place, the moisture, the shyness, and the particularity of things like bluejays--I remember
taming barn rats. I mean, I was fascinated by
animals and had early the thought to be a veterinarian, and actually by the time I was ready to
go to college I had a scholarship to Amherst
and to the University of Pennsylvania for pre-
veterinarian medicine. I then shifted to writing.
Or wanted to write, and so went to Harvard. Well,
people delight me, but again it's that damned
dilemma of wanting it all and not knowing yet--
I don't think yet in my life I quite know how
to do it. I like teaching, simply that teaching
gives me a formal structure that permits me an
intensive relation with other people. But otherwise in my habits I tend to, to need a space
around me that lets me go to bed now and then.
I mean, Allen Ginsberg makes a lovely remark
that when I get to town nobody sleeps till I'm
gone. I can't let anybody sleep because I don't
want to miss anything. I want it all, and so I
tend at times understandably to exhaust my friends
--keep pushing, pushing, pushing. Not like social
pushing to make a big noise; but you know, I
don't want to miss it. I love it. I so love the
intensity of people that I can't let anything
stop until it's literally exhaustion. And immediately, in relations with the girls I then knew
and loved. Again I'd want to push it right to
the end. I mean, it wasn't simply fucking them.
I wanted it all.

MacAdams: I've heard a lot of stories about your
fighting in those earlier days.

Creeley: That's when the confusions of how to
be with people became so frustrating and so
unavoidable that I would just spill. And also,
I think it had a lot to do with drinking, which
I did a lot of in those days. We were smoking
pot, as we called it, we were smoking pot pretty
continuously by about 194--. Let's see. I first
had use of marijuana in India, where I was in
the American Field Service. We were a barracks
at one point of about 40 men. We had all ages
and whatnot, and I think almost everyone in that
barracks was turned on almost all day long. We
were in central India. There was literally nothing to do. It was an incredibly awkward climate
for us. I mean it was very hot and so we'd be
sitting there sweating, and drinking was impossible. We drank as long as we could, until it
was a question of vomiting half the day in this
heat, and getting very damned sick. I had a
friend from Southern California who one day suggested to me that there was an alternative.
After literally bile for the last two hours
coming out of your guts, he said, "Try this."
There was nothing mystical. It was very, like,
"Here, have an aspirin." So we switched and
everything became very delightful. The food was
instantly palatable and life became much more
interesting. So that I remember, for example,
returning from England on the *Queen Elizabeth*,
being used as a troop ship returning Canadian
troops back to Canada and the few Americans
that were attached to British troops. And this
friend and myself, we were both smoking a lot
of pot on ship. In fact we used to get into the
toilet. About 15 or 20 people would be depending on this toilet, and he and I would get in
there and turn on, then sort of sit around.
There'd be this great mass of people standing
and waiting, banging to get in there. They
thought we were homosexuals. This was aided by
the fact that one night, I remember, I staggered
into the room, and you'd have these tiers of
bunks, and trying to get into my bunk, I climbed
into the wrong one. But we used to get up on the

boat deck, which was restricted, but we were
there anyhow. So it was absolutely silent and
isolate, seeing that whole sea in a beautiful
full moon. Just beautiful.

Well see, had I had the sense, or rather had
the situation been possible, I do feel that I
would have relieved much of my life had I not
been drinking in the frustration of social in-
eptness. And even to this day if I drink--I
mean up to a point it's extremely pleasant and
relieving and relaxing for me. But there comes
an inevitable point where my whole feeling turns
into irritation, frustration, and that's when
I fight. I mean, I don't think I ever fought
anyone except in that condition. I used to fight
in just sheer frustration, and a feeling of absolute incompetence and inability. And also people
were very belligerent during the forties and
fifties. We used to get into these ridiculous
fights. Happily I never got more than hit a few
times.

MacAdams: I heard you had a fight with Jackson
Pollock once.

Creeley: Oh yeah, a great meeting. Because he
obviously was having, you know, intensively the
same problem, with a vengeance. I'd been in the
Cedars Bar talking with Franz Kline, and another
friend of Kline's and Fielding Dawson probably
was there. We were sitting over at a corner
booth, and were talking and drinking in a kind
of relaxed manner. But I, again, you know--very
characteristic of me--I'd get all keyed up with
the conversation and I'd start to run, get the
beer, or whatever we were drinking, wasn't coming fast enough, so I'd, you know, I'd go back
to the bar, have a quick drink, and return to
the table and pick up the drink that now had
come, and I was getting awfully lushed, and excited, and listening, so I was literally at the
bar getting another drink, when the door swings
open and in comes this very, you know, very
solid man, this very particular man, again, with

this intensity. So he comes up to the bar, and
almost momently made some gesture that bugged
me. Something like even where he put the glass
on the bar, that kind of business where he was
pushing me just by being there, and I was trying to reassert my place. So the next thing we
knew we were swinging at each other. And I remember this guy John, one of the owners, just put
his hand on the bar and vaulted, literally, right
over the bar, so he's right between us, and said,
like, "Okay, you guys," and he started pushing
at both of us, whereupon, without even thinking,
we both zeroed in on him, and he said, like,
"Come on now, cut it out." Then he said, "Do
you guys know each other?" And so then he introduced us, and I was--God! It was Jackson Pollock!
So I was showing pictures of my children and he
was saying "I'm their godfather." Instantly
affable, you know. We were instantly very friend-
ly. And he was very good to me.

No, in those days, I remember, in the Cedars,
I had a big wooden handled clasp knife, that in
moments of frustration and rage--I mean I never
stuck anybody with it, but it was, like I'd get
that knife, you know, and I don't think I tried
to scare people with it, but it was like, when
all else failed, that knife was . . . not simply
in the sense I was going to kill somebody, like
a gun, but I loved that knife. You could carve
things with it, make things and so on. And so,
I'd apparently been flourishing it in the bar at
some point, and I remember he took it away from
me, John did, and he kept it and said, you know,
like, "You're not going to have this knife for
two weeks." And then he finally said, "Look, you
can't come in here any more," and I said, like,
"What am I going to do? Where am I going to go?"
So he would finally admit me if I drank ginger
ale only. Because I used to stand out front and
look in the window. And then he would let me
come in and sit, as long as I was a good boy
and drank only ginger ale. And finally he let
me have the knife back, because that knife was
very, very--I've still got one like it.

MacAdams: When did you start writing about art? I never saw anything before that Frank Stella piece in *The Lugano Review*.

Creeley: Well, through Pound's agency I'd come to know Rénè Laubiés, who translated some of Pound's *Cantos* into French--the first published translation of them into French. And Laubiés was an active and interesting painter. In fact I saw the first Jackson Pollock I ever really saw, in Paris at this friend's gallery, Paul Fachetti's gallery.

MacAdams: When was this?

Creeley: This must have been 1952. No, 1953. Up to then my relationships had been primarily with other writers. But I liked Laubiés extremely. It wasn't really the painting as something done that interested me. It was the painter, or the activity of painting I was really intrigued by. And so, at the beginning of that time I began to look at things. And then, because I was an American living in Europe, I was particularly intrigued by the Americanism of certain painters, like Pollock, obviously. And then I did have other friends, like Ashley Bryan, a friend of that time who was a painter. And so gradually I began to come into the relationship to painters that does become decisive. John Altoon, really, is the one who becomes very important to me because his energies were so incredibly--you know, the things he drew, made manifest in his work, were images in my own reality so to speak. And then Guston was extremely good to me. I mean, was very good to me in the sense that he was very generous with his interest and time. I was fascinated by the condition of life these guys had. Not simply that they were drinking all the time, but they were loners and they were, they were peculiarly American, specifically American in ways that writing, except for Williams and Olson and Duncan--I mean, they had almost you might say the iconography of the peculiar American

fact. And their ways of experiencing activity,
energy--that whole process, like Pollock's "When
I am in my painting"--that the whole condition
of their way of moving and acting and being in
this activity was so manifestly the thing we
were trying to get to with Olson's "Projective
Verse," the open field, you know *The Opening of
the Field*. And this was so much their fact, and
Duncan actually in his "Notes on *Maximus*" makes
very clear the relation to the painting that
he'd felt in San Francisco with the group there
--Clyfford Still and Diebenkorn and the whole
roster of people he had as friends. That, curiously, was far more fresh as imagination of
possibility than what was the case in writing,
where everything was still argued with traditional or inherited attitudes and forms. So in
the middle fifties anyhow, the painters, without any question, became very decisive for me
personally.

I was thinking of when I saw John Ashbery
two days ago. We were talking with editors and
publishers, and at one point Ashbery gave his
own sense of the New York School and its occasion. He said, "Well, first of all, the very
thing it is, the one thing that we were all in
agreement with, is that there should be no program, and that the poem, as we imagined it,
should be the possibility of everything we have
as experience. There should be no limit of a
programmatic order." And then he went on to
qualify his sense of the occasion, and why painters were to them interesting. Simply that the
articulation--range of possibility--in painting
was more viable to his sense of things than was
the condition in writing. And I thought, "You
know, that's literally what I would say. That's
precisely the imagination of the activity I had."

Now we were caught in various geographical
and habitual senses and thus for a time separated. You know, simply that we were intensely
involved with the way we were feeling the articulations. But at this point, I mean we are all
of us now roughly in our early forties, and what'

striking is that each one of us of this nature
has precisely the same grid of initial experience and proposal. And that we were finding
that statement, I think, or that experience of
it most articulately in the activity of painters
in that period--late forties to the early fifties.
John was obviously coming to it by way of the
French surrealists or the writers of that kind.
That's where he found, not only playfulness, but
a very active admission of the world as it's
felt and confronted, or met with. I was finding
it in jazz, for example. And that's why Charlie
Parker and Miles Davis and Thelonious Monk and
those people were extraordinarily interesting
to me. Simply that they seemed to have only the
nature of the activity as limit. That is, possibly they couldn't change water into stone.
But then again, maybe they could. That's what
was intriguing.

MacAdams: Well, when did you start writing about
painters?

Creeley: At Black Mountain I wrote a note apropos
Laubiés, which I think is the first note of that
order I wrote. Then, through the association with
Black Mountain, I became very intrigued by Guston and by the visual, what's seen in the world
and how all that can be complex. Because I'd
been so involved with the economy of words as
experience of sound and rhythm that suddenly it
was like having things open again as things seen.
And so I wasn't in any manner of speaking know-
ledgeable as to what this scene was as some continuity historically. Nor could I use the vocabulary of the usual art critic. But I could, in
Olson's sense, give testament, bear witness to
this. My notes were of that order. I thought,
I'm not arguing my experience of something as
an ego proposal. But all I want to do is to
say this has been seen in the world and this
is my experience of it. Not as argument, but
as invitation to come. You can see the relevance. We were making things. Not only of our

own imagination, which was after all finally
the point, but we were making things in the
materials particular to our own experience of
things, just as John Chamberlain was experiencing the particular fact of materials in his
world, e.g. those car parts, and seeing how the
imagination might articulate that experience;
I was trying to make do with the vocabulary in
terms of experience in my world. And neither
one of us had history. Neither one of us had
articulate experience of history, as something
we'd come through as persons the issue of.

I remember Duncan, a lovely moment when we
first met--he and Jess and Harry Jacobus had
come to Mallorca. I was in a rather dense and
difficult time in my marriage. Ann was away
for some reason, that is, was down in the city
shopping. We lived in a little house outside
of the city. You got there by a trolley and the
four of us were going back into the city to find
them a pension that they could stay in. We were
standing in this trolley with all the people
banging around us. I remember Robert--we were
all standing holding onto the straps and he
looked--turned to me at one point and says,
"You're not interested in history, are you?"
You know, and I kept saying, "Well, gee, I ought
to be. And I want to be. But I guess I'm not.
You know, I'd *like* to be but, no, that's probably true." That history, as this form of experience, is truly not something I've been able to
be articulate with, nor finally engaged by. So
that art is, somehow, as Williams might say,
the *fact* of something, but I did not have that
alternative experience of it as an issue of time.

MacAdams: Do you think that comes out of Pound?

Creeley: Yeah; I think Olson says Pound, by virtue of the brilliance of his ego and that proposition that there are men in time that he can
outtalk, or find as company for his own intelligence. And that there are, Olson suggests, only
two that can possibly beat him at it: namely,

Dante and Confucius. But that is still an issue
of historical experience. And by the time I think
I came alive in the world it wasn't a place like
that. Although I am a person, let's say, of the
generation that grows up in the Depression and
then the Second World War, I wasn't located in
it. By which I mean my mother had a civil ser-
vant job. We were living in a marginal manner.
I remember her salary in those years was about
$2,700 to $3,000. And that was adequate in those
years, I mean, it provided a stable economy. But
we were sort of in that curious faintness of being neither in the world as some daily struggle
with it, nor were we in any other world. We
lived in a curious limbo and so there was nothing to locate us historically. How we'd all
come to be in that house in West Acton was a
kind of wild absurdity. My father had gone there
with one imagination of it and my mother, for
example, had grown up in Maine. They were very
distinctly differing families. My mother's family were poor relations. Her mother had been an
Everett. And because of the charm of this young
woman, when young, her Boston relatives, or Cambridge relatives, had arranged for her to go
West with Wendell Phillips on one of his mission-
ary-like tours. And so she'd met Mark Twain, for
example. They got as far as St. Louis, I think,
and there was a young man in the company that
she was supposedly to be interested by. But in
the meantime she was in love with my grandfather
who was the oldest of six sons from a French-
Canadian Nova Scotia family. He'd gone to sea
at the age of twelve, after his father died, to
help support his brothers and his mother. And
he was the antithesis of this Cambridge experience. So she went back after and married him
anyway, and my mother, then, and her family
would be the issue of that fact. And my father,
on the other hand, was the only surviving child
of this Scotch-Irish farmer who was in the Massachusetts Legislature finally, because he happened to live on Belmont Hill on a very desirable
piece of real estate. So that as he stopped

farming, he then sold his farm to the interests
of that time and became quite wealthy, and seems
to have enjoyed a very happy sort of senility--
walked around Harvard Square in his bathrobe and
slippers. Gave all his money to the housekeeper,
obviously solace to him in his age.

I was the youngest son, my father had been
married twice previously--I have two half brothers whom I honestly don't know at all. One of
them changed his name in irritation and disagreement with my father's fact, and the other
never married and lives in Chicago. So that there
was a kind of blightedness one felt in their
lives. But these were two older brothers that
I never had really anything to do with. So I
didn't know where the hell anything was. My father had died in this way. Then other echoes of
the family were out there but never located.

MacAdams: Were your short stories written usually
in one movement like the poems?

Creeley: Right, and again that's why I say that
the kind of economy that Pollock was speaking
of was very real to me. That is, when he said,
"When I am in my paintings . . .," that way of
experiencing what he was doing was very known
to me, and that equally, I remember one time
in the fifties a conversation with Guston and
my first wife. She'd challenged him apropos:
"If you're painting this way, abstract expres-
sionism or whatever you call it, how do you
know when it's done?" She really was proposing
that he was in some way a phony, and that this
whole activity was in some way phony. And he
took the question seriously, and gave her a
very careful and generous statement of his own
experience of painting. His resolution to this
question as to how do you know when it's done
was to say when you are thus both looking at
and involved with this thing that's happening,
and you can't see any place where further activity is permitted, then you're done. I mean,
where everything has happened, what else is

there to do? And I knew again that that was precisely how I felt writing, that when I couldn't
say anything more, that was the end. Not I, again,
as ego, but when there was no more to be said,
more accurately, that was it. And I knew that
you thus continued writing and/or speaking until
no further possibility of speaking was there.
That was really the quote end unquote. Not that
you got to some point of resolution that you
imagined possible, but rather that you came to
the *end* of it. And I thought this was what these
particular men as Kline, or as Guston, or as
De Kooning—not De Kooning so much because his
formal procedure was rather different—but Pollock did. Absolutely. That they were not so
much experimenting, but they were both delighted
and moved and engaged by an activity that permitted them an experience of something, and
that they therefore were with it as long as it
was possible to be. And at some point it ended.
I mean *it* stopped, and they were thus pushed
out, or made to stop too, and that was it.

MacAdams: Didn't that come to be a problem when
you wrote *The Island*?

Creeley: Yes. I'd previously tried to write a
novel which I'd gotten so involved in as some
technical circumstance—I mean I was so involved
as to how you get from one chapter to the next,
or one segment to the next, that all the writing
became the articulation of devices, to have
something go on or continue—to move from A to
B. And the actual narrative per se is extremely
dull. I wrote about 90 pages, actually. I threw
it away finally. I was delighted that it all
went together. But I was bored by what it said.
So that, the most awkward thing I felt that I
had to get past was, "How does something go on?"
I mean, that is, "How does something start somewhere?" which, frankly, I feel might well be
anywhere. And *then* continue. I mean, what agencies for that possibility exist? The poems I'd
been writing, and the stories, had all been

intense seizures or absolutely centered, you
know, facts of emotional possibility, and involvement. And as soon as they exhausted their
particular locus, or particular center in that
way, they were done. That was the end of them.
It was like a seizure, or a fit. But now one
wanted to have something go on. I was intrigued,
obviously, by Olson's *Maximus*, and I was certainly intrigued by Allen's *Howl* and *Kaddish*.
And I was intrigued by Duncan's "A Poem Beginning with a Line by Pindar." By that kind of
possibility in Pound and Williams in *Paterson*
and *The Cantos*. I wanted something that could
go on. I was intrigued by Olson's reference to
The Cantos as "a walker"--something you could
take a walk with daily, and have as experience
of daily possibility. And I know there was
enough emotional center in that circumstance
of the first marriage, but I didn't want to
talk about it as though I had the decision of
it. I didn't simply want to tell what happened.
I wanted something I could now enter into, in
1960 I guess it must have been, that I could
begin with. And I knew that the emotional confusion still hanging in the experience of it
was enough. If I began speaking in this experience of something, I knew it would have enough
energy to make something happen. But I was ter-
rified. I said, "God, you know a novel is maybe
200 pages. On page one how can you imagine the
possibility of page 200?" And it was Bobbie actually who said "Don't." I mean simply begin with
what is, and then see how it is extensible or
how it permits something to continue. This too,
I got from Allen--Allen's sense that *mind is
shapely*. That you don't have to think about
thinking in writing in that way. You permit the
experience of thinking to manifest its own condition. Bobbie said, "Simply start writing. Not
start as some order. But begin with what is, and
then see what happens. I mean don't worry about
page 200. Don't worry about its being a novel.
Don't worry about what kind of plot it can have.
Don't worry about anything of that order. Just

begin with what seems a particular possibility, and write outward. Write from there." And it worked. Then I did give myself sort of hand-holds. Not in any sense of subject, but rather in the economy of the procedure. I know, for example, a story for me was five pages. This both satisfied me that there was enough of it. And that equally I felt that five page balance gave me a locus that was very useful.

MacAdams: What about the size of the paper?

Creeley: That changed. I mean at times the page would be bigger. Living in Spain I used legal-size sheets so that that would change the length of the stories. It wasn't a formula. It was just a habit--in the same way that, say the choice of paper and pencil or pen or typewriter were. It was part of the instrumentality. Just so, that sense of a five page context. It would be like buying a particular size of canvas. I felt very at home with that size of canvas, so to speak. I wanted to work in an economy of state-ment that had to do with a range of five pages. If you look at the manuscript you'll find that the chapters are all about five pages. The next question was, "How shall these be distributed, these five page pieces?" Then I thought, "Well, in fours." Four is a number that actually feels very comfortable to me, and yet has a variety of possibility within its own nature. Like one and three, or two and two. Or simply four. So that I can feel that that makes a viable balance. And so I then designed the circumstance as five chapters to each part. There are four parts. Four main parts. And then each chapter is in an economy of five pages in length, with five chapters to each of the four parts. And five times four is twenty, which is the number of chapters in the book. Which is sort of back to two again. I thought this was sort of--not cava-lier--I remember trying to explain this to people, who would say, "Well, how did you do it? What did you have in mind for the plot?" And I said,

"Well, you know, four times five." And they
thought I was a nut or something. But, I remember one time talking to Douglas Woolf. I said
I was using fives and fours. He said, "Do you
know that last novel I wrote?" I think he was
speaking of *Wall to Wall*. He said, "That's written in an economy of three, two, one." But it's
written in that term of duration.

The problem is that in speaking of writing,
usually if one says something like that, the
literary critic, so to speak, is completely
confused. Because he thinks of the organization
of writing as having to do with symbolization,
or with the development of character, or with
plot. But he forgets that what's most interesting in that circumstance is what I would call
the numbers of it--the phasing and the balances
that have to do with number condition. Not with
any assumption--I mean, hell, the novel isn't
so much *about* life. Either it's manifestation
of the possibilities of life, either it's life
itself, or else it's something that I certainly
don't want to carry like baggage along with me.
So that phasing, just as it may occur in film-
making, where it's equally a case, that is you
can get a phasing of the relation of images in
a one-two, or one-two-three pattern that really
has much to do with how that enters, then, into
the experience of seeing it, and in the case of
a novel, of reading it. That four times five is
an experience of not so much only a quote order
unquote, but equally, I think, right back to
that sense of the scale of the particular axis.
Things like that. Those paintings of Pollock's
which are distributed along the horizontal, as
opposed to those which are vertical. That just
so, in numerical balance, you have a curious
and insistent initial experience of how things
are going to come together. Anyhow, that was a
great piece of information to have in hand when
I was writing. I don't think I knew it consciously, but it felt good. It felt very appropriate.
And it permitted me use of previous experience.
That is, the stories. So that, instead of thinking

of writing the novel, I thought of writing a
sequence of such takes. Then I began to experience, as they continued, their interworking. I
remember finally getting to the end of the book,
and I'd literally written it in four weeks. I
wrote in an intensive manner. By which I mean
the book was written effectively. Although
those four weeks occur in a two year period.
When it was all done, I remember sitting down
and reading through the whole thing, and just,
I mean literally being gassed that it had all
this interweaving that I had in no wise intended. I hadn't intended it. I hadn't thought of
it. But in the writing it, it was part of the
economy of writing it.

My only argument with people who think things
previous to experience is that that becomes an
awkward prohibition of what can happen in the
actual activity. Again painters are relevant
insofar as painters will tell you momently that
to paint what you know, as Kline would say, is
a bore to oneself. To paint what someone else
knows is a bore to them, so one paints what one
doesn't know. And the point of that is, the
painting becomes a process of realization. Not
simply an habitual insistence that this which
we had known anyhow is still the case. Like
"Yeah, Mother's still there. Father's still
there. The house is still there." This is very
boring information. At least in writing, for me,
it's the kind of information that I, at times,
deeply and truly depend upon. But in writing I
want to be free. I want to range in the world
as I can imagine the world, and as I can find
possibility in the world. Of course we are within limits, as Olson would say, but it's to find
where those limits are specific that's interesting. Pound, by the way, has a lovely note
apropos Henry James--"Pushing his limits in
order to realize what they are." That is, he
points to certain instances of James' writing
where one feels, with hindsight, that the particular nature of James has been distorted in
James' intent. That he's tried to do something

which is peculiarly unsuitable. But how does
one know, as Pound says, until one thus pushes
limits to experience where they actually are
occurring.

So that novel was great. That novel opened
up a great deal of possibility for me. I remember Duncan saying, after he'd read it, "This
really changes the whole formal occasion for
you. Both rhythmically, and in the order of statement you previously had." And I think he's right.
I think it permits poems like "The Finger" to
be written.

MacAdams: Do you think it took this many years
to actually occur?

Creeley: Yeah. I'd come in that time previous
rather like a man who has decided that one thing
is the case in all application. That there is
one way to write. Or one way permitted to him
to write. Short intensive poems. Short intensive
stories.

MacAdams: Didn't "The Door" explode that at all?

Creeley: "The Door" was something that anticipated the explosion, let's say, but didn't realize it. I mean it realized it in its own fact
of being a poem of this kind, but it didn't
give me a continuity. The poem wasn't so much
not characteristic, although I would then have
thought so; but it came from experience I was
extremely tentative with. I know the lady, as
it literally says. But this way of moving around
with a reality was something I hadn't previously
been able to do. Let's say that there are impul-
ses to this longer, or more various way of experiencing things. There are indications that
this is hopefully going to be the case. That is,
I was thinking of poems like "The Rose." Or
poems like the final poem of that book, "For
Love." But both those poems are rather recapi-
tulations of previous experience. Although they
get to terms of that experience that are being

realized as the poem is written. "For Love" is
really a kind of statement of "Look, we've lived
in our lives in this way, and we have had this
experience of them." It's the kind of note one
would like hopefully to write to one's wife,
or someone thus sharing life with us, saying
"This is our life," like Williams' "Perpetual
Mobile--The City." What's interesting about
"The Door" is that it's moving into new occasions of experience, and by the time, hopefully, I get to writing, like "Anger," I mean
that's not the rehashing of previous circumstance. That's an opening mode. And honestly,
by the time I get to "The Finger" now, now the
information is transformed. In the writing, and
in the experience that the writing is getting
to.

And that's what was happening in that damn
novel. Because, hell, I knew what my life
with this particular woman had been. I mean,
we'd come to a divorce. I was separated from
my children. I mean, if someone asked me, "What
happened to you, Bob?" I'd say, you know, it
was a mess. But in writing all that assumption
of what had happened began to be transformed.
And I began, not so much only to know myself,
but John became a character, like they say.
Not merely myself as some historical fact of
something, but John became an experience that
was new to me. I didn't know who the hell John
was. And suddenly, John became someone not
merely quote Robert Creeley, but rather became
this wild viable extension of some imagination
of someone by him or her self. Really, by the
time I got to that novel I had a wild experience of how you think the world. That this man
gave--John, I mean. He's not me as some kind
of photograph of a previous reality or identity.
He's now in the world as much as I am. People
objected that the woman, Joan, is not given
substantiality. Again, they're arguing a previous attitude toward prose as though a novel
were to be fair to all of its people. And give
everybody a chance. And the fact of the book

is that it's the experience of thinking as
creative reality; and hell, in that reality
Joan had no substantiality. In fact, the very
quote point unquote of the book is that this
way of being in the world ultimately makes
unreal all else that is in the world. It's like
a cellular system in Burroughs' sense expand-
ing to the point where it subsumes and distorts
all other event, I mean literally, it tries to
imagine--it's like that old business of God.
Trying to imagine not only that God is, but
that one is God. As though all creation would
now be the fact of thinking.

A few weeks ago in Vancouver I had a reading,
and I was trying not nicely or sweetly to make
known to this young group the *horrors* of thinking that thought itself can possess the world.
And I read that last chapter of *The Island*. I
really was wanting to insist that this is what
you can do to yourself, man, if you think *that's*
an interesting trip. And that's why I kept writing "I want to get out of my mind." I mean, I
didn't want a deracination of the senses, but
I wanted to get out of that awful assumption
that thinking is the world. I was thinking how
things have shifted, literally, in my experience
of the world from that time of the forties when
mind was thought of as the primary agent of
having place in the world. I think that came
probably from that sense of getting out of the
whole nightmare of the Depression by being able
to think your way out. And isn't that characteristic of Roosevelt's administration that
there enters into American government in political circumstance a sense of expertise--the
ability to think your way out of dilemmas; that
is, to deal with the national economy by thinking of a way out. I mean, even the Second World
War was a mind game. You confront one agency--
isn't Hitler, for example, thinking the world
is one thing; and then there are those obviously involved thinking it another.

But it honestly, to my mind, isn't until the
sixties that people begin to, as Allen Ginsberg

would say, come back into the experience of
their own bodies as primary, and to realize
that the mind is physiological. It is not some
abstract deity that can be apart from the physiological moment of existence. I was thinking
of that sense of Williams' of the interest in
the mind and body as one. I think that if we
want a center for experience now, it is this
sense, that the mind and body are one. This to
me seems one aspect of the revolution, in terms
of human experience of itself, that is the human
experience of him or her self in the world. It
seems to me that we have moved from that duali-
ty that absolutely informs all my thinking as
when I'm a kid, for example, that, you know,
"the mind is to discipline the body," or "the
body is to relax the mind." "You get drunk in
order to relax your thinking. You think in order
not to get drunk." It's a weird tension and the
torque that's created by that systematization
of experience is just awful. Just incredible.
It can *whip*. You know I called a book *The Whip*.
And that's why, that's why the title. I don't
think I consciously went and said, "What's a
word for this particular kind of experience,
but that--I know--I wasn't to my own knowledge
a sadist or a masochist. I knew that something
whipped me constantly in my own experience of
things. Something was really, you know, WHAM,
WHAM, slashing and cutting me. And yet if I
walked down the street I knew that nobody was
coming at me in that fashion, so where in the
name of heaven was all this taking place? Well,
it was taking place in my thinking. Someone
would hand me something pleasant, possibly, of
whatever nature, and my momentary way of experiencing that was to imagine all that it couldn't
be. Why am I being given this? What's the trick?
Well, thinking asks "What's the trick?" That
doesn't mean we have to be thoughtless. Or, it
would take extraordinary discipline to be thoughtless, as Gary Snyder would testify. But it's
very interesting that all of the people of my
generation, so to speak, have each one of them

come to some resolution of this dilemma with
all the energy and all the particularity of
thinking that they can bring to it. When Allen
speaks of his ability presently to have a good
LSD trip, what he's also saying is that he has
finally been able to relax, not only to relax,
but to get beyond the thinking that was the
bad trip all the time. Or that when Gary is
drawn to Zen, it's again to exhaust the mind's
exercise of its will upon the body's nature.

MacAdams: When you tripped did you have any
problem with that?

Creeley: I had momently one, when I entered
upon the seriality of language. I remember at
one point I did enter the dualism which is yes-
no, that binary factor. I felt that momently
it was going to be absolutely awful. I had just
said something such as "this is the case" and
I suddenly had an intensive experience of "this
is the case - this is not the case - this is
the case . . ." and then the identity of myself
and all persons. It was not an ego loss, but
it became--it was like seeing a vast checker-
board--that kind of alternating situation.
Then I just, by grace of something, stepped
out of it. Just stepped out. Then in the second
experience with it, last summer, that blessed-
ly never entered. And all through that second
LSD experience I had Donovan's "There is a
mountain." And I had equally a pleasant younger
friend, and we'd taken it about two in the morning. We had a fire burning, and we were in
an idyllic place in New England, at least in
this way--fresh, and the woods. A beautiful
morning. It would have been hopefully, anyhow,
but I mean it was beautiful. The day broke
clear and fresh and dewy, and there was all
this moisture in the trees and the grass--those
spider webs of moisture, and it was just idyllic. And the whole tone of the house became
apparent in it. The children were without any
consciousness of what we were in. They had

obviously neither concern nor interest nor
knowledge that we were on LSD, like they say.
But somehow the whole information of this feeling went through the whole house, so that the
girls had walked down to a store maybe a mile
away and bought us a chocolate cake, which
they gave us at one point. And they also spent
about an hour and a half that morning making
a necklace of pine cones which they gave Bobbie. The cats and our dog were, you know, almost ravenous for us. The cats were crawling
all over us. It wasn't just our hallucinating
and thinking they were. They were with us every
moment--intensively, rubbing up against us and
purring. From the fire in the fireplace that
light, beautiful light, then seeing the dawn
come up back of us as the room began to transform into the . . . So that "The Finger" is
directly, you know, that information.

Now in this form. I remember that business
of, and this woman--this beautiful primordial
experience of woman, in the guise of my wife;
but equally her image floating between the
moments of birth--as girl-child as they say,
to the most cronelike, the most haggish. Just
crazily--all the guises of woman. All that
Graves, for example, in rather didactic fashion
tries to say is the case. I mean, he's right,
certainly he's right. But it's not a hierarchy.
It's an absolute manifestation throughout all
realms of existence in this woman figure, and
yet that woman is woman. She's unequivocally
woman. It was absolutely delightful. I thus
"jiggled the world before her made of my mind"
and I thought, "That's the delight. That's what's
meant when people say morphology, or men make
form--man is form and woman is essence. Of course.
But the pleasure is how the world comes to that
point, and the delight is--that's like the dancing in the delight of thought, not the agony
of thought as fixed pattern. But it's the delight
of thought as a possibility of forms. When you
get lost in those forms, for Christ's sake--
when anybody proposes that those forms are

necessary or moralistically correct or the only forms, *then* it's a nightmare.

DOUGLAS FLAHERTY AND
JAMES BRADFORD: AN INTER-
VIEW WITH ROBERT CREELEY

The then editors of Road Apple Review *inter-
viewed Robert Creeley at the University of New
Mexico on the Friday before the presidential
election (November 1968), which unreal event
was the starting point of their discussion.
From political disaffection in general, the
emphasis soon began to focus on the situation
of the black community. Then someone brought
poets into it and the interview concluded with
where poetry is.*

Interviewer: During your poetry reading a few
weeks ago you said that you were not going to
vote, that voting is an artificial situation--

Creeley: I think that at this point it is. Simply that the content of choice with respect to
the particular candidates we're offered, at
least in the national election, the context
that they are a fact of, is no longer pertinent
to present life. For example, a friend of mine
spoke of a group of students coming to him at
NYU to get his support for the protest of the
firing of a particular teacher there, one of
the black community people. He said no, I won't
march, because the point is that what happens
if you get this man reinstated? You are simply
continuing the structure that fired him. Now
as far as this national election is concerned,
I don't know if I will vote or not at the last
moment. I feel that it is a very specious election.

I don't think that the election of either Hum-
phrey or Nixon will change the nature of the
structure. I don't know that that structure is
going to be so simply changed anyhow. It may
be naive to continue to depend upon an elec-
toral system such as we have for the changing
of an environment that we are finding increasingly intolerable. In other words, it may be
not only inappropriate but impossible that the
present political structure will change its
mind, and that, of course, proposes revolution
as the alternative.

Interviewer: We saw a bit of this in Chicago,
but do you think that the political machinery
in America is proving intolerable to anything
like a majority of Americans?

Creeley: I'm interested in a contention of Buck-
minster Fuller's, namely that we receive many
stimuli apropos our relation to a governmental
process, e.g. how we feel about political persons, how we feel about the war, etc., but the
provision for our ability to qualify and/or to
respond to these stimuli is very, very small.
We are given an opportunity to vote every four
years nationally, and then say every two years
locally, but in terms of all the stimuli we are
flooded with about the conditions of the country, cities, riots, etc., our ability to act
and to respond is extraordinarily limited. And
I think that people feel extraordinarily frustrated that their attitudes towards public
events and/or events which obviously concern
them, are not being given any occasion for
actual representation. That's why they personally feel frustrated in voting, because the
kind of attention to the kind of circumstance
that they really would like to see the case is
in no way represented.

Interviewer: About the information bombarding
us through the mass media, isn't another source
of anger and frustration the credibility gap?

The distortion and/or the withholding altogether
of information vital to the lives of each of us?

Creeley: Yes, as a friend was saying this morning, it seems to be arguing that human consciousness is not *one* consciousness, but rather is seg-
mented--you know, like *my* intelligence, *your* intelligence. It's arguing that there is some dif-
ferentiation within the human species that makes
information particular to this person and therefore not particular to that one. As though the
whole experience of the human species couldn't
be thought of as a whole consciousness which
they, in their multiplicity, possess.

Interviewer: Apparently there must be a safety
valve somewhere. At present, these frustrations
don't seem to be felt by the great majority to
be intolerable.

Creeley: The majority seems to regard a political agency as something which it is going to
change tomorrow. Our gods are gods of the future.
We don't have gods in the sense that the Greeks
did--we don't even have what you would call
loosely a Christian God. Our gods are the possibility of the future and so we are continually rushing to enter this future and then we're
continually disappointed because the moment that
it becomes the present, it loses its possibility.
We rush through it, exhaust its contents, and
then leap to the next that's coming. We're poised
on that endless moment that we think is continually approaching us and all the good in the world
is there in that next instant, and when that next
instant is this instant, it all turns to ashes.
    The black community in New York, at least as
I understand it, has never really wanted a situation in which their children were being bussed
to other parts of the city. The white liberal
middle-class imagination feels that in order to
gain a coherence among the city's peoples, it
is very necessary for children of various classes
and backgrounds and ethnic habits, let us say,

to all share the same school. The black community understood that this was not necessarily
happy. That if you take a kid from a poor environment and put him into context with people
who have altered environments which are better
or worse you really destroy what possible coherence he has. That the coherence most to be
valued is the coherence that's initial in the
group itself. That if you want to help schools
you don't take the kids out of the neighborhood and send them elsewhere, you give them
increasingly articulate teaching within the
circumstance. And that some kind of imagined
melding of all these conditions into one ideal
citizen who understands and is tolerant and
respectful of every condition just doesn't happen. So in the situation in New York what's
happening seems to be an increase of local coherence. When you know where you are you don't
have that curious hangup with where other people
are. You can enter their situation much more
easily. You may find it strange, but it's when
you feel threatened or feel that their situation
is about to overtake or transform yours that you
become threatened.

Interviewer: Why then does the white community
feel threatened by the possibility of the black
community developing its own style of life?

Creeley: Well, for one thing, the content of
the black community is not known. I mean literally not known. I remember talking to British
soldiers and personnel in India prior to the--
I was almost going to say the emancipation of
India--who asked, "Can you imagine what it's
like to live in this country where you are a
member of a 5,000 person military group sitting
on this number of people?" Well, I think a lot
of white people feel that they have been--wil-
lingly or not--sitting on the black community.
That they have been literally committing themselves both to ignoring and to making use of
the fact of this population block. Understandably

they feel pretty uneasy because they don't know
what the experience of that has been for the
Negro. They have very decisively avoided any
consciousness of what that experience was like
to live. The situation is not unlike that of
Germany after the war. It was the national attitude that no one really knew what was happening
in the concentration camps. People weren't trying to absolve themselves from responsibility,
they were really saying what was probably the
truth, that they didn't know. They had committed themselves not to look. There are thousands,
millions of whites in this country who have
committed themselves not to look at the condition of the Negro, and they feel an extraordinary dilemma now that they are being brought to.
They are being even more brought up against it
because the black community is not looking to
them for solutions. That's a real shift. If the
black community were looking to the white community for solutions, then the white community
could find a place in the exchange.

Interviewer: Don't you think that the content
of the Negro's experience is being communicated
by black authors and teachers, and by programs
like the recent CBS series on "Black America"?

Creeley: I don't think so because it seems to
me that what the white consciousness can experience as a basis of life decision is still
in no way involved with the black community's
fact. It sounds like I'm arguing racism, but
I'm really not. I'm trying to gain respect for
the literal condition of any person and I think
it is therefore necessary to resist any kind of
lumping together. The black community is resist-
ing this too, and in fact, I think what's been
both unexpected and even to my sense brilliant
about the black community's constitution of its
own forms and acts is that they have not proven
agreeable to white invitation, they haven't
accepted that invitation, and because they
haven't they continue to have their own dynamic.

There must be thousands, millions of rituals
particular to the black community which the
white community doesn't even see.

Interviewer: So communication, right now anyway, is impossible?

Creeley: At the community level, yes, probably
so. Some drastic social changes are in order . . .
I think every intelligent man, in every field
of activity feels that the world has changed
more in the last ten or fifteen years than it
has in the previous 5,000, and if this is the
situation of continually insistent proposal,
then someday something has to happen commensu-
rate. You can't go on simply saying tomorrow's
another day and we'll just get along.
    A friend was telling me about an article he
read in, I think it was *Art News*, which was
protesting the fact that the artist, the painter,
for example, works for an apparent elite and
doesn't seem to be involved with the people.
If you were to take this statement seriously
what would you do? A painter reads this article
which informs him that he is not sharing his
activity with the people and must instantly
stop doing it the way he is doing it and paint
for the people. What is this? What does he do?
Get assigned as a billboard painter? Hire out
at the nearest ad agency? So my friend was saying that the very coherence that the arts have
had seems to be derived from the fact that they
can intuitively continue their own coherence.

Interviewer: This touches on something you were
saying the other day about objectivity in poetry.
You said you didn't like objectivity because it
doesn't permit you to share the intimacy of the
experience which the poem records.

Creeley: I think there is a need to see what
the fact of oneself in the world is. There is
that kind of objectivity. There's the dilemma
that comes from being so personal, so personally

involved and so tentative about a further condition of experience that one never really knows
where one is more than to say "I like it," or "I
don't like it." But to me art itself is the ob-
jectification of my own experience. Also, I
don't see the point of writing as though another
experience were more interesting than one's own.

Interviewer: In your case, is *the* experience
that leads to a poem a special kind of experience?

Creeley: Yes, a poem seems to come from some
fact of experience or context of experience
that cannot be withheld or subjugated to some
intention.

Interviewer: What about formal intention? Some
forms of poetry seem to me to disguise the poet's
relation to his experience and to impose affects
on it which are external to it.

Creeley: Well, the poem is an event. It's like
Williams says, "How to get said what must be
said? Only the poem." What does he mean by that?
I think what he's involved with is the fact that
in an art you can realize what you have as experience of the world, consciously, but equally
in so far as you are an agency for saying something.

Interviewer: I'm not sure I understand. If a
particular experience gives rise to a poem,
isn't it a kind of corruption for that experience to be formalized in a way that brings
other gestures to it?

Creeley: Writing is like someone giving his address as such a street in such a town in such a
country in such a hemisphere, etc. The point
is that if you say anything you have immediately
created a situation in which all the world can
occur. If you say the word *yes* and begin to
qualify why that's the case, you only stop at

the end of the world. If you begin with a feeling that prompts you to say something, then the
experience of *what* you were saying would tend
to take over. Like I tell this woman that I love
her. Well now, because I have that as experience,
or want to have that as experience, *how* do I
love her? Immediately the assertion becomes the
condition in which something always follows and
I'm not going to get on to the next thing until
I understand what I have at each point.

[*Road Apple Review* I:1-3, 1969]

THE WRITER'S SITUATION

In 1969 the editors of New American Review *invited Robert Creeley to participate in their symposium on "The Writer's Situation" by replying to the six groups of questions given below.*

Question: Why do you continue to write? What purpose does your work serve? Do you feel yourself part of a rear-guard action in the service of a declining tradition? Has your sense of vocation altered significantly in recent years?

Creeley: "Because it's there to be written," as William Carlos Williams said. I don't really know if there is more reason than that, in relation to some sense of purpose or intent. There are clearly things I've wanted to do in writing--specific forms I've wanted to try, as a novel, for example, or diverse ways in which an active *seriality* might be manifest. But the primary occasion in writing is a situation I've never been able to design, even when I've much wanted to.
    Thinking then of why one continues--that's equally inexplicable, except that it is, literally, an active possibility for me, in my life. It keeps happening, and the way the world then enters, or how I'm also then known to myself, is a deeply fascinating circumstance. Charles Olson makes a lovely point, that "we do what we know before we know what we do," and that really is the delight in writing, that much

happens one has no conscious information of until it is there, in the words. I'm not thinking here of some sort of do-it-yourself psycho-
analysis--that's of no interest to me--but a
deeper fact of revelation I feel very actual
in writing, a realization, reification, of *what
is*.

The tradition to which I relate comes, as
Robert Duncan would say, "from a well deeper
than time." It's not yesterday's news one is
concerned with. However one thinks to qualify
it, the fact of being a poet teaches one that
it is not an ego-centered occupation but a
trust one had really no thought to undertake.
But there it was. Suddenly. One morning. With
the birds. I'm trying to say that poetry comes
from a *tradition* far more complex and rooted
in the human condition than any one "time" can
define. Better to consider Konrad Lorenz's
sense of tradition as he speaks of it in his
book *On Aggression*--the intuitive economy of
human experience, biological and environmental
in this case.

As to my sense of vocation--for a long time
I was very tentative about saying in any forth-
right manner that *I* was a poet. It seemed extraordinarily presumptuous. But again, it's
not a vocation one can earn, however one respects the responsibility of this literal "cal-
ling." In any case, being a poet is something
I can acknowledge more clearly in my own nature
at this point. It seems a consistently present
reality, although I respect a qualification a
friend, Max Finstein, once made: that one is a
poet in the act of writing, not otherwise.

However, I realize the nature of this question has really to do with a sense of *literary*
tradition, and vocation as some form of *professional* occupation, etc. I've always been an
amateur insofar as I loved what I did. Olson
said that Melville had over his work table the
statement: "Be true to the dreams of thy youth."
I respect that commitment deeply. If anything,
I feel a deep blessing and good fortune in what

my "vocation" has given me as a sense of my life.
Saying that--it seems suddenly a little conveni-
ent, in a way, but I do feel blessed by life,
no matter that at times it is difficult and painful.

Question: Do you believe that art and politics
should be kept apart? Has this belief changed
or grown more complicated during the past de-
cade? What influence has the politicalization
of life during this period had on your work?

Creeley: Having come of age in the forties (I
started college the summer of 1943), "politicalization" was, it then seemed, so much a part
of that time I don't know that it seems more so
now. Perhaps it's some sort of weird sandwich
one is experiencing, with the blandness of the
fifties intervening, the bread being the forties and the sixties. But having been in some
ways active in the Henry Wallace party, also
having been taught politics by the YCL while
still in college--it doesn't seem to me that
life is now more political. It certainly isn't
quite as didactic, let's say, as was the member-
ship of the PAC--or any friends then involved
with postwar Marxism. I don't think there is
quite the same insistence on the "right" and
"wrong" ways that there was then.
     Possibly political agency is regaining an
active context. But really the advanced younger
people of this moment are, if anything, *post*-
political, just that the available political
agencies seem to them so bankrupt. The militant
part of the black community might be the one
active revolutionary group still intent on political possibilities. I know that many of the
young showed an active commitment to Eugene
McCarthy's leadership in the circumstances of
the last election, but I question, even with
reluctance, that that had initially to do with
political occasion or possibility. More, I
think, they wanted renewal of a kind of *presence*,
in public life, possessed of a demonstrable

integrity, even one apart from the usual conditions of political activity. They wanted
someone to be literally there--and this was,
curiously, not the case either with Kennedy or
Nixon. Both were finally part of a system the
young have every reason to distrust, as, god
knows, the elders might equally.

Obviously the disaster of the national commitment to the war in Vietnam is the largest
"political" counter of the past few years, and
it served to energize political agencies in
every sense. But again, I'm very intrigued by
the hippie culture, so to speak, and its decisively apolitical character. It's as though
a very deep shift in the conception of human
relations and use of the environment were taking place--and indeed I very much believe that
it is. We've come to that time when, as Williams said, we must either change our "wishes"
or perish. I don't feel that present insistence
on ecological problems is simply a new game. We
have literally to change our minds. In this
respect, drugs in the culture have really two,
among other, clear possibilities: (1) either
to reveal a oneness in all manifestations of
life-form of whatever order, and thus change
the mind by that revelation (certainly the most
useful information to be gained from taking
LSD); or (2) to kill anxiety, to lull intuitive
perception of inherent peril, to simply get out
of the "world" one is actually in--and in this
respect the elders are as committed to this
use of chemical agency as any of the young.

In any case, I don't see that art and politics, or that order of present experience involved with the post-political, should all be
kept separate. I don't see how they can be.
One can't, perhaps, entirely respect an art
committed to propagandizing or to a use of life
not clearly initiated in its own activity. But
when men and women are outraged by political
malfeasance, it's hardly likely that their art
will not make that quite clear.

As far as my own work is concerned--I've not

been able to write directly to a purpose of
political involvement. It's not given me in
my own nature to be able to do so, but I hope
that I've made clear where I stood nonetheless.
I hate the outrage of human beings that present
political acts now effect. One must protest
them--they are literally against life itself.

Question: What are the main creative opportunities and problems that attract and beset you
in your work? Which movements, tendencies,
writers, if any, do you find yourself identi-
fying with or supporting? Which ones do you
oppose?

Creeley: It's difficult to qualify just what
"creative opportunities and problems" are primary. Just that something does come to be
said, is an opportunity of very great magnitude.
Too, poetry as I've had experience of it is
not, finally, at the service of other conditions
or orders of information, however much it may
serve them once it exists. Olson says that art
is the only true twin life has--in that either
is not to a "purpose" apart from the fact of
themselves. They don't *refer*, so to speak.
There's no *excuse*.
    The "problems" occur when one loses his way
in such possibility, muffs or misuses the nature
of what's given. It is, again as Olson says,
something as actual as wood, or fish, that one
has to do with. It's not in the mind in some
sense that one can now exercise a discretion
upon it--thinking about it in some privileged
way. To the contrary, there is a feeling that
adamantly does insist one is being told something and had better get it right the first
time, else there won't be another chance. One
is told *once*. For this reason I find it hard
ever to revise--"re-see"--just because the initial seeing has to be responded to with all the
ability possible because I'm not given another
chance. It's very like seeing someone you do
respond to in the instant, and having thus the

choice of going home and thinking about it, or
making that response a manifest act. I agree
with Robert Duncan that choice is recognition
--not a debate between alternatives. So if one
doesn't know "what to do," given such circumstances, clearly there's nothing really to do.

Otherwise I'm not much concerned with either
creative opportunities or problems. I love a
particular poem by Kenneth Koch, beginning
something like, "Thank you for giving me this
battleship to wash . . ." Thank you for giving
me *creative opportunities*, i.e. I wonder what
a woman would say to that.

"Movements, tendencies, writers . . ." There
is a *company*, a kind of leaderless Robin Hood's
band, which I dearly love. I'm sure there is
even a horn to summon us all. There is no company dearer, more phenomenal, closer to my
heart. A few weeks ago I happened to spend
the night at Allen Ginsberg's farm, and coming
down to the kitchen in the morning, met with
Allen's charming remark, "All the poets are up!"
Which very truly we were, Lawrence Ferlinghetti,
Gregory Corso, Allen, and myself--while five
others also there slept on.

Whether learned by intuition or by act, one
comes to respect and love that company of
writers for whom poetry is, in Bob Rose's phrase,
"active transformation," not a purpose, not discretion, not even craftsmanship--but *revelation*,
initial and eternal, whatever that last word
can mean to one whose life is finite. Consequently I both identify with and support--and hope
I might be permitted the company of--any man or
woman whose experience of writing transcends
some sense of its value as money in the bank,
or edifying addition to one's identity, etc.
None of the so-called Black Mountain writers
wrote in a literally similar manner. That is,
Olson's modes of statement are certainly not
mine, nor are they Duncan's, nor Denise Levertov's--and so on. What was, then, the basis
for our company? I think, simply the insistent
feeling we were *given* something to write, that

it was an obedience we were undertaking to an
actual possibility of revelation. Which to
say one might own would be absurd.

What I find abhorrent is any assumption that
one has gained the *use* of writing as a private
convenience, to me the ugliest of all attitudes.

Question: Has writing entered a "post-modern"
era, in which the relevance of the great modern
writers (Joyce, Eliot, Mann, Faulkner, et al.)
has declined? If so, what seem to be the literary principles of the post-modern age? If not,
what principles of modernism are still dominant
and valuable?

Creeley: Supposing "modern" to define the primary consciousness of a decisive shift in the
conception of *reality*, which becomes increasingly clear toward the end of the nineteenth
century, then one may feel that that consciousness is now a general condition in human experience. The world cannot be "known" entirely.
Certainly it cannot, in the way men are given
to live in it and to know it, be "perfected."
In all disciplines of human attention and act,
the possibilities inherent in the previous conception of a Newtonian universe--with its containment, and thus the possibility of being
known--have been yielded. We do not know the
world in that way, nor will we. Reality is
continuous, not separable, and cannot be ob-
jectified. We cannot stand aside to see it.

Writing, and all of the arts as well, have
entered the altered consciousness of men's
situation in the world. One might speak, possibly, of "the modern" as the first impact of
that realization in the arts: Eliot expressing
both regret for previously possible order and
recognition of the new experience of how the
world happens--simply what takes place. Yeats,
in a late note on modern poetry, understandably
with frustration, speaks of modern poets as
asking us to "accept the worthless present."
If one thinks then quickly of Samuel Beckett's

use of that "present," "where to be lasts but
an instant where every instant / spills in the
void the ignorance of having been," a measure
of the change involved is apparent.

Much that the modern writers got said seems
to me still of great relevance. Both Williams
and Pound--or Lawrence, Stein, H.D., and many
others also--point up the dilemma of what may
be called individual sensibility in an environment insistently generalizing all circumstances
of apprehension and decision. That problem
hardly seems solved. However, what is at first
feared as a loss of coherence--felt most in
the loss of history's authority--starts to become less that as other situations of experience occur. High and low art begin to melt
as historical valuations blur. All being *now*,
all that *is* there has possibility. The ego's
authority tends to relax, and conceptions involved with proposals of "good, better, best"
also lose ground. Most interesting to me is
the insistent presence of what has been called
the *chance factor* in the activity of all the
arts of the past several years. Whether in
"happenings" or in the music of younger com-
posers like Cornelius Cardew, one sees that a
discipline, so to speak, is being gained to
discover a *formal* possibility in a highly variable context of activity. It may well be that
"beauty" is simply being returned to "the eye
of the beholder," but what that eye expects to
see is nonetheless much altered.

Still it does seem that terms such as "modern" and "post-modern" are habits of art history.
One tends to use all that he can get hold of,
and I don't know that one "time" is thus distinct
from another, in the actual practice. *Here* is
where one seems to be.

Question: Has there been a general collapse of
literary standards in recent years? Are you
conscious of a conflict between your past standards and your present ones?

Creeley: I remember an incident, like they
say, involving a critic I much respect, Warren
Tallman, and an Englishman, in a radio discussion of Jack Kerouac's *Big Sur* for CBC. Warren
was plugging for Kerouac's genius in being able
to make so articulate and substantial all the
data of the senses. What impressed Warren was
the fact that when some thing or activity was
spoken of, one's experience of it was extraordinarily vivid. The Englishman, however, felt
that some canon of literary form had been broken. When Warren pushed him to qualify just
what "standard" he was referring to, the man
hedged, unable actually to state it--then said,
"Well, we know enough to know these standards
exist, even if we don't know what they are."
    Kind of a wistfully moving point, actually.
But I'm extraordinarily wary of *any* "standard"
not the direct result of an active experience
in the practice of the art involved. Or as
Olson puts it, "telling me what in the instant
I knew better of," and this is not by any means
an egocentric response to "rules" imposed by
taste and opinion, that have nothing to do with
the nature of the language and all the possibilities therein. Pound quotes Remy de Gourmont,
"Freely to write what he chooses is the sole
pleasure of a writer"--and I agree with that
utterly. "Standards" are only interesting in
relation to the possibilities they recognize.
In the forties I felt them arbitrarily restric-
tive and dominated by the practice of criticism
apart from the practice of poetry itself.
    So far from feeling there has been a collapse
of literary standards, I feel there has been a
reconstitution of them in the practice of
writing itself. Think of the victories actually
won: relaxation of censorship in the use of
specific words, admission of serial order as
a complex and diversely organized phenomenon,
a riddance to all senses of "poetic subject,"
poems *bien fait* to some dull mold, and so on.
The list is happily a long one. In short, I
think that such standards as poetry involves,

and they exist unequivocally, are again the
issue of the practice--not a viciously para-
sitic *addendum* put on the practice of poetry
by men in no wise committed to it.

My past standards continue to be my present
ones. I permit myself possibly more freedom
now--not by a relaxation, but in the broader
range of perception I am able to respond to in
writing, in the degrees of emotional condition
I find I can speak. *Man standing by his word*
--Pound's translation of the Chinese ideogram
for *sincerity*--stays as my own measure, but I
have begun to apprehend too the complexity of
that situation. It's not a simple honesty, etc.

Question: Has literary criticism and journalism kept pace with, and faith with, the best
fiction, poetry, and drama produced in the sixties?

Creeley: A lovely novelist we know, world-
famous no less, writes on a Christmas card just
received: "For Christ's sake keep up the good
work and don't be sidetracked by Christmas or
the goddam reviewers who are ugly people . . ."
As far as I'm concerned and speaking particularly of the situation of poetry, there is *no*
correspondence of any interest to me between
the activities in contemporary criticism and
that poetry I am myself most engaged with. Even
if one considers a particular critic of intelligence, Richard Howard, who is also a writer
of poems, the score is still lousy. In his
book, *Alone with America*, "Essays on the Art
of Poetry in the United States Since 1950,"
there are gaps I so deeply question that the
book itself becomes a fine instance of *mandarin*
writing--i.e. an "entertainment" of "sensibility." And he is, in my own estimation, perhaps
the best. Where "journalism" may be in any of
this, I simply don't know. Reviews are either
so tardy or so absent one can hardly consider
them as "keeping pace." A fellow wrote recently to tell me he'd been asked by *The Nation* to

review my collection *Words* for one of their
coming issues. The book was published in 1967.
Pieces, a subsequent collection of poems, was
published last August, and possibly that might
be reviewed in the far, far distant future.
But really, one hardly depends on it.

The point is, if one meets with an exceptional critical intelligence--e.g., Kenneth Burke,
D.H. Lawrence, Edward Dahlberg, Ezra Pound--
then *that's* the point, not "literary criticism."
Joshua Whatmough says, in a book called *Language*,
that literary criticism is just an exchange of
opinion and has no authority in relation to the
activities it criticizes. That cheers me up.
When younger, I was not "criticized" at all.
Now older, it seems I rarely do things right,
or five years ago I did them right, not now.
As for literary criticism "keeping faith"--
I didn't know it had faith to keep. If one is
thinking of men active in the arts making notes,
etc., then the whole question obviously changes.

December 21, 1969

[*New American Review* 10, August 1970]

MICHAEL ANDRÉ: AN INTER-
VIEW WITH ROBERT CREELEY

---

*Michael André came to Bolinas in the summer of
1971 for this interview with Robert Creeley,
which he later published in his magazine* Un-
muzzled Ox.

André: What have you been writing lately?

Creeley: Actually I've not been writing very
much at all except for one thing very new to
me, a radio play. There the interest has been
that I didn't actually 'write' it, I composed
it using a tape recorder and simply improvised
the sequence, the statement, let's say. I had
the imagination of two characters, one being
the sense of "I" as a designation of person,
and one the sense of "you" as an invocation of
person, so that the "you" becomes various--it
goes through four or five changes of identity
--whereas the "I" is the constant.
    The play was commissioned by Westdeutscher
Rundfunk and will be broadcast this winter in
German translation. And that really is the most
active thing I've done in the last three or
four months.

André: Do you consider *Pieces*, your most recent
book, an open poem like the *Cantos* or *Maximus*
or *Paterson*?

Creeley: I'd had great respect for what Olson
and Duncan had got hold of, let's say, with in

Olson's case the *Maximus Poems* and in Robert's
the whole sequence of *Passages*. It gave them
a range and a possible density of statement
that was very attractive. As a younger writer
I had been most able to work in a small focus,
in a very intensive kind of address, so that
I depended on some kind of intense emotional
nexus that let me gain this concentration. But,
literally, as my life continued and I continued to live it, I really had a hunger for something that would give me a far more various
emotional state, that is, the ability to enter
it. And also I wanted a mode that could include,
say, what people understandably might feel are
instances of trivia; that is, I really respect
Duncan's sense that there is a place for everything in the poem in the same sense that Williams
says--"the total province of the poem is the
world"--something of that order in *Paterson*
somewhere--the sense that poetry isn't a discretion, that it is ultimately the realization
of an entire world. So that I felt the kind of
writing I'd been doing, though I frankly respected it, was nevertheless partial to a limited emotional agency and therefore I wanted to
find means to include a far more various kind
of statement through senses of writing I got
from Olson and Duncan. Equally from Ginsberg,
who could lift, you know, some apparent instance
of a very insignificant order into a statement
--not verify or enlarge it but simply find a
place for it. *Pieces* really became a kind of
open writing in the sense that it was composed
in a journal as daily writing. Sometimes weeks
would go by, obviously, and nothing would be
written.

But the point is there was no need to have
every poem titled, there was no need to draw a
distinct formal line around every poem as
though it were some box containing a formal
statement: I simply let the writing continue
almost as a journal might. And when the time
came to publish it, I simply used the chrono-
logical sequence of its writing and let, say,

three dots indicate that that was the end of a
day's accumulation, and the single dots most
usually indicate divisions in the writing as
it's happening, as I was sitting down to do it.
In other words, I wanted to trust writing, I
was so damned tired of trusting my own opinion
as to whether or not this was a good piece of
poetry or a bad piece of poetry. That kind of
dilemma really faded for me during the fifties
and sixties. In the forties it had been a large
argument:--what is a poem? By the age of forty
or forty-five I thought if I don't know, it's
obviously too late to learn. So I simply want
to write in my own pleasure and forget that
kind of signification that formal criticism
insists on.

André: You've mentioned in your prose writing
at various times that you don't have a "larger
view," but that this is all right. Do you think
perhaps this form, which implies an acceptance
of "process," is a larger view?

Creeley: In some ways it is a larger view. I
don't think it solves everything--simply that
one's life goes on and the diverse conditions
of it at various points of biological age begin to give information themselves--I'm now
forty-five and I've lived in various relationships and various, you know, literal physical
places in the world and it's impossible for me
to feel that there aren't those literal changes
in my own person. My nature seems to stay fairly
anchored but a larger view accumulates as well
as finds itself in some attitude towards the
world. I thought the world was very large when
I was eighteen, I thought it was so large I
could never find a way in it. Then at times I
thought obviously I can't live in the whole
world so I'll simply stake out a place and hang
on. That's about as absurd as planting a flag
on the moon. If you've got that far you've got
a lot further than you think.

André: *Pieces* doesn't have any national political discussions as do the larger poems of
Lowell and Denise Levertov. Why?

Creeley: Why? Simply, the information of political attitude and/or conduct hasn't yielded me
materials that I can make use of as a writer.
I feel that writing is primarily the experience
of language, and the diversity of contexts, and
the diversity of changes and significations.
I'm frankly and selfishly interested in the words.
I'm interested in discovering what words can say.
One dilemma for me in the political context has
been the insistent didacticism of attitude, the
locked mind that enters almost immediately with
any political statement, the insistent rhetoric
which places the words in an extraordinarily
locked condition. Particular writers, such as
Olson or Ginsberg or Levertov or Duncan or Bly,
find it possible to use this condition of feeling as material, and to discover a language
that can be this material. Myself, I haven't
been able to do that. I've done a lot--not a
lot--I've put my own commitments on the line,
I think, by holding draft cards and by reading
for the Resistance and I've had no intention
not to state myself politically, but this
hasn't entered my poetry. It's almost as if
I've given so damn much to that idiot war I'm
damned if I'm going to give it my experience
of words.

André: One of your volumes of poetry was called
Words and one noticeable trait of your poetry
is that words which seem to have a common signification after a while take on an irreducibly
puzzling air, for example, the word "form."

Creeley: Yeah.

André: It's used in so many different contexts;
would you care to give a definition of one of
these words?

Creeley: No, no I wouldn't [*mild laughter*]. "Form" has such a diversity of contexts possible to its proposal that it really depends I think on the occasion in which the word is finding place or is being given a place. I remember a lovely statement Wallace Stevens made years ago in reference to writing: "there are those who think of form as if it were a derivative of plastic shape." There are indeed a lot of writers who think of form as something you give the poem, that you take and shape it the same way you might shape a piece of wood to form a boat or whatever. I question that. Imposition of form upon words is always a problem for me --I've known men brilliantly to do it--Zukofsky, for instance, at one point in *A* gives a brilliant use of this kind. But form for me is something that's found in activity.

André: In *Pieces* . . .

Creeley: One last note on it. The only definition of form that really stuck in my head for years is really an instance, an example which I think is one of the very few interesting definitions of anything. It's a lovely quote that an old friend named Slater Brown once gave me. He said it was a definition from Blake though I've not ever found it. It simply goes "Fire delights in its form." That to me is the context I'm involved with.

André: In *Pieces* you have incredibly brief sections--I can't think of one offhand--which are almost concrete . . .

Creeley: --it
                       it--
                          for example.

André: Yeah.

Creeley: Right.

André: Very brief poems.

Creeley: Right.

André: What do you think of concrete poetry,
do you think it's arbitrary form?

Creeley: No. I think it involves what language
has had as a visual context. The world has
had the experience of seeing words for three
or four hundred years as public events like
billboards, posters, broadsides, whatever. It's
not at all untowards to think that a poetry
could evolve that was interested in words as
a visual, as opposed to an oral, state of experience. And the poets I've known most interested in that are Aram Saroyan, a brilliant
poet of this order--of any order for that mat-
ter--and Ian Hamilton Finlay. In both cases I
think they have done extraordinary things with
this possibility. As for example Aram Saroyan's
very short poem--

> eyeye

It gives a lovely reification of the eye, of
the eye's activity, of the two eyes' activity.
I think it's part of the possibility of language.
I think it's useful.

André: Similar to what you do with words, in the
sense of stripping them of their commonness, you
also take situations . . .

Creeley: I try to find their commonness--I don't
want to interrupt you so argumentatively.

André: That's okay.

Creeley: I'm really trying to discover their
common essence wherein they relate in an extensive way. For example, a friend here, Tom Clark,
recently did a lovely book which is simply
lines or quotations from Neil Young's songs and

they compose an extraordinary book. I was also
talking rather sadly in that sense to a friend
here, Kitaj, who had used quotations from Zukofsky's poetry in a print that he did in honor
of Zukofsky's poetry and Louis was upset that
the words occurred without proper acknowledgment; there was a proper acknowledgment because
the print made clear that this was a homage to
Zukofsky. At the same time Kitaj, because of
his own habits as a painter, hadn't thought to
write for copyright, etc., etc., so Louis was
irritated and questioned the use of the words
blah blah blah. A person like Tom Clark would
think "who owns words?" Words are common. If
you go swimming, you don't say: this is my drop
of water and that's your drop of water. Obviously you're swimming in a common ocean. I really
respect these young writers like Tom or Lewis
MacAdams or John Giorno who don't worry about
quoting in that awful sense. Everybody in my
generation was involved with being original,
scared to death they would sound like somebody
else. Some of these younger men can sound like
anyone in the world and I think it's delightful.
Tom Clark, be it said, gives me the most accu-
rate criticism of *Pieces* specifically in a poem
called "A Sailor's Life" three or four issues
ago in *The Paris Review*. That's criticism in
Pound's sense of the use of the occasion that
the initial poem springs from. And I have been
very interested to see that that book's criticism has really consisted of people who know
how to use the formal modes got to there. Not
people who thought they understood what it
meant. But the people who could demonstrate by
their use of it that they were with its contents.

André: In your poems particularly prior to
Pieces you tend to suppress the circumstances
surrounding the poems, you tend to make your
poems into general dramatic statements.

Creeley: Right.

André: Is that because you disapprove of personal life in poetry?

Creeley: No, the writing I've done at times has
been felt to be so exclusively personal that
people questioned its relevance to others. Even
the landscape where the events were occurring
was not that actively present. They didn't have
a clue to its occasion except that obviously I
felt it. One old friend felt that *The Island*,
for example, was a private apology for a state
of feeling, a relationship, and therefore questioned its use to other people. But I know what
you mean. I wanted to strip away as much adden-
da as possible, to get it down to the nitty-
gritty of the particular circumstance of feeling. I didn't want to argue that, o.k., that
was true in Mallorca, but what would it be like
in Boston? Or, of course it was true at four
o'clock in the afternoon, but what if it were
eight o'clock in the afternoon? I was trying
to get not merely a "universal" occasion but
I was also trying to strip away all that kind
of qualification. I say "I heard" and you say
"Well, you heard, what about me hearing?" You
know, that kind of argument.
     And then again moving into writing like
that in *Pieces* and really beginning with information in *The Island* involved a continuity of
statement that was really very new to me at the
time. *The Island* was my first "long poem"; it
was the first piece of serial writing that went
on for many days, weeks, and so forth. It taught
me a lot; it made me impatient with other forms
of writing for quite a while. *Words* is an attempt to think of various other ways to move:
towards the end those very short poems like
Pieces (in fact "A Piece") begin to signal at
least in hindsight what the writing was trying
to get to, that is, a far freer context of
statement. I really felt that if an elephant
were not standing on your foot or if all your
children hadn't momently died in some awful
fire, then you really had no right to say anything.

André: There was a debate in *The New York Times* a few months ago between Richard Howard and Allen Ginsberg.

Creeley: I heard about it. Unhappily I didn't read it--oh--happily I didn't read it.

André: I was wondering who you'd side with in the debate, or if you'd side?

Creeley: Ginsberg. Well . . . yeah, sure. Wasn't it questioning the circumstances of the National Book Award?

André: Yes. Howard was upholding a "poetry of excellence" so to speak.

Creeley: I think a poetry of excellence takes care of itself. If one's at a time when world consciousness seems to be shifting in its dispositions towards experience, I think it's time indeed to acknowledge the resources of a far more extensive modality of statement than I feel Richard Howard does, despite what he gets to in *Alone with America*. In very real response to his ability, he's written perhaps the only essay on Gregory Corso's work that shows an active perception of Gregory's abilities. I think that's to be commended, but he is a critic.

André: Some people feel hostile to Howard.

Creeley: He's a strong man. He's got a very articulate head and he works. Most people feel hostile to people actively working.

André: You wrote a beautiful poem on Allen Ginsberg in *Words*.

Creeley: I've been deeply moved by his compassion for other human beings and his commitment to being with other human beings in the world. Characteristic of Allen, he's been recently at hearings here in the city, a federal commission on drugs, particularly on marijuana, and apparently he's cut his hair and he's wearing a blue suit and a felt hat, beard and mustache all gone, and when a *Times* reporter asked him what he was doing he said he was "in drag." Which the *Times* misreported as "he said his previous state of dress was a drag." Speaking of politics, Allen is very alert. It isn't just that he wants to change his image but when his image becomes so habitual an appearance for other human beings, he's no longer interested in it; not if he wants to be active politically.

André: Your poetry has a kind of hip/beat air to it like Ginsberg; you deal with hallucinations and drugs and things like that.

Creeley: I saw a comment in a recent anthology to the effect that I was some sort of hip Emily Dickinson. Lovely thing. I thought she was pretty hip to begin with. I've been fascinated by diverse states of feeling, be it sitting in the sunlight or smoking marijuana; but I've certainly not used drugs in any conscientious manner.

André: Sometimes I know you're describing a state of feeling but I can't quite gather, practically speaking, what is going on. For example, there's a story, "The Dress," in which a man continuously imagines a cavern into which he will bring his wife and her friend. What brings him to this powerful kind of . . .?

Creeley: I don't know. There's a cave across the street in that hill and at times kids come in here to borrow matches so they can go in the cave and look around. Now that's a literal cave back of a hardware store across the street and that cave is a very explicit experience: obviously to leap upon that as though it involved necessarily some symbolism--one symbolism for boys and another symbolism for girls--this might be some awful estimation of where they were in the cave. But that cave has a fascination

for them. And if you live in a way that makes
you uneasy in the so-called mundane world,
think of all the imaginations of enclosure,
the retreat someplace where you can be sane,
secure, you know, the whole business of wanting to get back to the womb, blah blah blah.
Caves have a very initial sense of security.
I was writing the story not in a sense of symbols, although obviously symbols are there,
but in a sort of--surrealist would be my own
estimation of that story's context. I wanted
to state in surrealist terms the particular
isolation I was feeling in the intensity of
these two women's talking. My place became the
imagined cave under the floor, and when I took
them into it, I took them into the intensity
and privacy of my own experience, with its own
containment. Then I was using caves I knew in
Mallorca. They have these wild stalagmites and
stalactites which, you know, are obviously insistent sexual presences. So that the whole
vocabulary sort of melted in this story which
was really about the dilemma of the relation
to a literal wife and her own senses of insecurity and the reassurance happily this other
friend was giving her; and the dilemma of the
dress and "who was she?" It's always fascinated
me, that sense of the dress as becoming to you.

André: How Creeleyesque.

Creeley: I did not say it, it's what it said.

André: You recently seem to have gotten to another *state* of feeling--I don't know--in "Numbers," some of those little contemplations of
a number seem mystical. Would you describe them
so?

Creeley: That poem was written on the suggestion
of a friend, Robert Indiana. He at first asked
if he might use a selection of poems that were
published to accompany this sequence of prints,
of numbers from one to zero. I thought, wow,

what would be far more interesting from my
point of view would be to try to write a sequence of poems involved with experiences of
numbers. In some halfhearted sense I looked up
texts on numbers and got some information that
way but it was so immediately so scholastic
and scholarly in tone that I couldn't use it.
I was really using something as simple as "what
do you think of when you think of the number
eight; is that a pleasant number for you?" I
was thinking of sayings like "two's company,
three's a crowd." I was thinking of the groupings implied or the imbalances implied or the
odd numbers, the even numbers. Then other writing, like the last part of the zero sequence
called "The Fool," is simply a quote from a
text by Arthur Waite called *A Pictorial Key to
the Tarot*. I just looked at that because to me
it was a beautiful estimation of the experience
of nothing.

André: One of the other poems in *Pieces* is
titled "Canada" and it's only four lines long.

Creeley: It's a quote.

André: It's a quote?

Creeley: Heard on the radio, I believe. The CBC,
no less. We were listening late at night in
Buffalo and suddenly we were tapped into the
history of the national emblem, etc., etc.,
and just those kind of grand proposals gave
me the poem. I just like the way it went together.

André: Irving Layton was connected with Black
Mountain?

Creeley: Really he was basically connected with
Cid Corman and myself and Olson as part of the
Origin group; an issue of *Origin* is devoted
in part to Irving's work. And we in turn were
contributing frequently to a Canadian magazine

called *Contact*, which was mimeographed and put
out by Ray Souster and Irving and Louis Dudek.
And that coincidence, that would have been in
the early fifties, that coincidence of acquaintance and interest was really strong. I published a book of Irving's called *In the Midst
of My Fever* and I published another book for
him called *The Blue Propeller*. I was really involved by Irving's work; I thought it had a
lovely, beautifully sensual lyric quality and
I liked him indeed. That was before he was the
national poet.

André: In the first issue of *Black Mountain
Review* there was to me very interesting attacks
on Dylan Thomas and Theodore Roethke. Do you
still stand by those attacks?

Creeley: Yes. In fact again Duncan and I were
talking only yesterday about the situation of
another young friend, and why it is something
is persistently unclear in his work. As Duncan
put it, he hasn't yet come to his person, his
person is not given him in poetry. There are
those writers who really feel the primary activity they're involved in is getting something
said, e.g. "there are eggs in the icebox" or
"it's raining outside" and they are interested
in conveying a content of that order. But that's
what they're involved with words for: to get
those things said. There are other writers who
want to live in their words, like Olson says
"we who live our lives quite properly in print,"
who want, literally, the experience of realizing themselves in writing, not only to realize
themselves but to realize the potentiality and
extension of words as a physical event in the
world. One of the incredibly nostalgic and poignant situations of Roethke's writing, for example, is that I don't ever feel he came to a person. He looked with deep insistence and longing
to find that person, himself, but that person
never emerged. I mean it's as if you need to
say, will the real Theodore Roethke please stand

up? It's intriguing, he's not realized.

André: What about Thomas?

Creeley: Thomas frankly to me has always been
an extraordinarily muzzy writer. Some years
ago Graves offered a reward to anyone who could
explicate a poem of Dylan Thomas. I think that
was a specious request, but I can well understand his impatience with a kind of smarmy
longing that just wanted to hear sweet sounds.
Unhappily Dylan Thomas's work contributed to
a sense that poetry really doesn't do much of
anything except sound rather melodiously in
the background; he unwittingly was used as an
axe to cut off people who were, you know, I
thought far more valuable to writing.

André: Talking about magazines, it often struck
me as curious that since there are masses,
literally masses of English students and would-
be poets that magazines like *Poetry* are never
mass-circulation magazines.

Creeley: Well, it may be an awful fact that all
of us in various ways have got to realize, that
literature is not what it used to be. What I
respect increasingly in students is the ability
to stop encapsulating an attitude towards writing in the sentimental sense of evaluation:
this is a good poem, this is a bad poem. People
can speak of writing more ably in terms of lin-
guistics, because the habit of literature has
become awfully sentimental. It's like the habit
of art history; it tends to get awfully vague.
"English Literature" doesn't mean anything
frankly. When I taught in Canada I was teaching a freshman English class in which no Canadian author was required. That's a terrifying
estimation of English literature as far as I
can judge. I think of people out of Saskatche-
wan, not sentimentally, but those were real
people with a real life event. They'd come
from an extraordinarily real place, the plains,

and they'd come in that lovely old-fashioned
respect for the educational possibility and
they met with the most bleak, scared, spine-
less subservience on the one hand to the British core of taste and on the other hand to the
American economic efficiency, and they fell
through the slats.

André: Why did you drop out of Harvard, or do
you care to say?

Creeley: I was unable to complete a course in
analytic geometry I'd taken as an entering
freshman; in the meantime I'd gotten married
and gone to India and Burma as an ambulance
driver; in other words, so much had changed
in my life. It wasn't that I was stupid in
terms of mathematical condition or concept.
I never had any trigonometry, so I was doing
analytic geometry longhand, so to speak; I
was doing all that calculation in my head. I
could keep up with it in the eagerness of being an entering freshman but not being a jaded
and disillusioned last semester senior. Also
we'd moved to Provincetown and I was commuting
from Provincetown to Boston on one of those
lovely old boats like the S.S. *Steel Pier* or
S.S. *Chauncey Depew* and arriving in Boston
stoned out of my head because they served
liquor on the boat for three hours. I'd lose
my books and I was failing so finally the dean
called me in and said, "Look, you have two in-
completes and a failure in your three courses
and I advise you to withdraw until things are
more stable and you come back and finish the
last semester." Well, I just never came back,
I never really had occasion to. Ten years later
I thought of doing it, I had left my first marriage and was thinking of the teaching I had
happily found to make a living and I had no
degree of any order, and I was being asked to
produce one. I eventually went to the University of New Mexico as a graduate student and
got an M.A. there. The B.A. from Black Mountain

was a euphemism. I told Olson about my dilemma
and he said, well, you taught the courses,
therefore you should have credit for them--
we'll give you a degree. It served. I needed
something that would specify I had a particular academic ability.

André: Jack Nicholson's film *Drive, He Said* . . .

Creeley: I could tell you quite a bit about
Mr. Nicholson's film.

André: Tell us.

Creeley: Briefly, just after it was shown at
Cannes . . .

André: I don't know if everybody knows . . .

Creeley: Jeremy Larner's novel *Drive, He Said*
uses as motto, and takes as title a line from
a poem called "I Know a Man." Jeremy is a
charming, pleasant man; I was charmed that he
liked the poem well enough to use it in that
fashion. So three or four weeks ago we were
sitting in this room and the phone rang and it
was Jeremy from Hollywood saying they'd just
completed a film of the novel and the poem is
quoted, or more accurately misquoted, and was
this all right with me? I was sort of charmed
and I said, great, you know; again, obviously,
thinking of Tom Clark's sense, why not? Another friend however said, that's ridiculous man;
to subsidize Hollywood? So this friend's agent
very generously took on the matter for me. The
point is, very briefly, the film is a flop.
One is not going to get rich on this film or
any like it. Finally the whole thing drizzled
out; they had no permission to use the title;
their previous authorization certainly did not
include using the poem in the text of the movie. That's show biz, or rather that's business.
To take the thing to court would be both bleak
and absurd. I have no final word but I'm sure

a small "settlement" will eventually be made
plus a free ticket.

André: The film interpreted the important line
of the poem as being "the darkness surrounds
us." And an academic wrote an essay on the poem
as a put-down of those who think the darkness
surrounds us. Do you agree with either camp?

Creeley: I don't know. Brautigan told me there
was a review in *Time* magazine which quoted the
poem saying the movie was awful but the poem
held up pretty well. He also told me, thinking
of how quickly things enter public use, there
was some report of a swimming competition that
began with the headline "Dive, She Said." I
can tell you very briefly and quickly what "the
poem means to me."

André: Maybe you could read it again.

Creeley: This poem has had a very curious history. Just before I do read it, there was a
lovely time once, I think in the early sixties
or late fifties, when writing of mine was not
usually picked up for critical discussion; in
some kind of wild supplement in the London
T.L.S. there was a weird discussion of this
poem and a poem of Larkin's, "Whitsun Wedding."
They were talking about the Christian attitude,
and so on, and the discussion proposes that
the "I" of the poem is probably Jesus Christ
and the John of the poem is probably John the
Baptist. It's the most incredible distortion
of any intention I felt in my . . .

André: Probably got somebody tenure though.

Creeley: Incredible. "John" is almost a hier-
archical name for me, I've had very good friends
named John. I was thinking of one very specific.
Instantly two friends occur to me: John Altoon,
a painter who was a very close friend, a very
very decisive friend for me, and another friend,

also a sculptor, John Chamberlain, who's equally a dear friend. "John" became a name for an
order, of not merely *machismo* or some kind of
campy sense of manhood, but almost a hierarchi-
cal name for some measure of friendship, and
a man of that condition.

André: The figure, who I take is largely autobiographical in *The Island* . . .

Creeley: Yes, John becomes both myself and the
imagination of a man. It's like John Doe but
it isn't, it's like John Bunyan, it's a hier-
archical name.

> I KNOW A MAN
>
> As I sd to my
> friend, because I am
> always talking,--John, I
>
> sd, which was not his
> name, the darkness sur-
> rounds us, what
>
> can we do against
> it, or else, shall we &
> why not, buy a goddamn big car,
>
> drive, he sd, for
> christ's sake, look
> out where yr going.

One thing, the lovely paradox about the movie
and everything else is that syntactically the
line reads for me

> why not, buy a goddamn big car,
> drive

and *then*

> he sd, for
> christ's sake

André: It is misquoted.

Creeley: Yeah, it's a misquote. The poem pro-
tects itself. It didn't even get the syntax
straight. Not that I made it simple for them.
I like the impulse of "drive," *then* "he said."
I could have said, period, you know

>   drive. He sd, for
>   christ's sake

But "he" doesn't say "drive." I think someone
who reads it in the actual impulse will recognize that he isn't saying drive, that's the
person who's proposing, "why don't we buy a
great big car and drive"; it's the "I" of the
poem who is saying "why don't we get out of
here" the car being one imagination of how
we get from where we're stuck, hopefully to
someplace where we won't be. It's the friend
who then comes into it, who says, "take it
easy, look out where you're going because you
can't get out of things by simply driving
around." "The darkness surrounds us" was just
the kinds of senses of confusion and muddiness
and opaqueness that people obviously feel in
their lives. And this was one sense of "let's
get out of this and do something else." The
friend just says "look out where you're going
because that impulse is obviously human and
to be respected but you don't really do much
that way." "I know a man" in the sense, like,
I know a man who can fix your roof or like that,
a *useful* man to know.

André: You mentioned Richard Brautigan. Are
you fond of Brautigan's work?

Creeley: Yes indeed. I think especially fondly
of his prose which I didn't take to when I
first read it, in Canada actually, when I was
in Vancouver, and when I had generously been
approached by Don Allen to help with the editing of a selection of prose which was called

New American Story. Among the materials considered that Don suggested were *A Confederate
General from Big Sur* and *Trout Fishing in America*. The latter had been turned down by x number
of publishers in this country, and Don finally
published it. So Don was obviously committed
to the writing. I was in a very serious mood
in Canada, I don't know why or wherefore, I know
one reason was, I had been writing *The Island*
and I just couldn't read Brautigan's prose in
that state of mind. I mean I read it, I read
both novels, this was about 1961, 2 or 3 and
I thought they read like some wild shaggy dog
story, which in a very real sense they do. But
I was too uptight in my own sense of what writing "should" do so that I couldn't read them,
and I vetoed them--to my everlasting shame because I really dig them. They stick in your
head.

André: He seems to be influenced by you.

Creeley: No, I don't--you know who's the actual
mentor for Richard's writing, the actual close
mentor for his writing is Jack Spicer; he's a
very particular student of Jack Spicer's. Speaking of influences, Richard and I were talking
about possible editions--I was offered the possibility of editing a selection of Walt Whitman. I had a choice of various authors and the
one I frankly was first drawn to was Thomas
Wyatt, but then when I actually looked at a
text of Wyatt's I realized to fill a book would
be pretty difficult; there were extraordinary
poems but the range was pretty limited. There
are at least a dozen friends I would figure
more able, like Ginsberg or Duncan or Zukofsky,
to do an edition of Whitman, but since I've
got the chance, boy that's what I want to do.
We were talking about this circumstance, and
Richard said he would like to do an active
selection of Stephen Crane's poetry, or of
poets from the thirties who are largely ignored in this country, like Kenneth Fearing.

André: Yes, I like Fearing.

Creeley: I don't think Richard is interested in so-called melopoeïa, he said he wants to say things using the simplest possible unit of statement as the module. The last novel he's published, *The Abortion*, I think is an extraordinary book. I think he's a very particular American writer, he has all the eccentricity of an American of a real order. He's not topical. I was at a friend's house who was reading Tom Wolfe and we were talking about Ken Kesey, and about the time Ken Kesey was at Millbrook at Leary's place and Tom Wolfe's report of the whole impact of that visit; it's a very jazzy and interesting way of saying it, but it's a beautiful journalism. Whereas Richard's writing is initiatory; it's the *primary* statement in his writing that I deeply respect. And his poems again stick in my head; I don't think there's any sense in saying, are they as good as Ezra Pound's? There's no point to that.

André: About predecessors, *The Island* seemed to me to be more like D. H. Lawrence and your short stories seemed to me to be more like James Joyce, which is another of those . . .

Creeley: Lawrence was a really deep influence on me as a younger man. I really thought he was an extraordinary prose writer, *and* poet-- the modality in poetry was less of interest to me--especially the short stories, things like "The Fox" and "The Captain's Doll." I really loved his stories. Then Williams had a deep impact on me as a younger writer. Apropos your mention of Joyce, I can literally remember reading *Dubliners* as a junior in high school and the impact that made on me as a *feeling*: incredibly sad. And Stendhal had a like impact --it's hard to say, it's such a meld--Dostoevsky was like God Himself when I was younger. Those were all writers of prose.

Pound is literally instruction. His *ABC of Reading* and a book I used practically as a bible when I was younger, *Make It New*, published by Yale, those books were extraordinarily interesting to me. All of Williams' writing is interesting to me.

Among the so-called Elizabethans, I remember Andrew Crozier asked me what edition of Campion I used and if I was using manuscripts or some edition, and I thought, all I'm using is an anthology that includes some Campion. I remember Campion had a deep impact, I don't know why, just one or two lines that really hit and stuck.

. . . . . .

André: How has success hit Richard Brautigan?

Creeley: He's a loner. He grew up in difficult circumstances as a kid; the family had no money and I think his father worked as a fry cook; they moved all around that part of the country, the Northwest, looking for work, two or three months in one place, living in furnished rooms or hotels or motels. Richard came to the city deciding to be a writer, rented a room, watched his money dribble away, he rarely left the room somewhere in North Beach he told me, and then there was a day he decided he had to leave. He hawked everything, got what few possessions he wanted to start hitchhiking, and had a lovely epiphanal moment when he was going through some mountain pass almost at midnight with snowy fields and moonlight and realized only eight hours before he had been in a situation where he thought his life would be more fitly ended. He has had extraordinary response in the last few years which he obviously enjoys. But, for example, when a group in New York approached him with the possibility of making a musical out of one of his novels, guaranteeing him something like $5,000 a month for starters,

and giving him complete disposition as to what
the production should be, Richard really came
on the dilemma that that would mean New York
productions, Chicago productions, San Francisco
productions; it would mean that the actual audience he has in mind for what he writes would
basically be excluded; they don't live in New
York; they certainly can't pay prices of that
order. He realizes that very possibly in ten
years he will be a has-been in this vast topical meat-market, so he simply stakes himself
as long as possible on present income. He does
live in this $75 a month apartment; he told me
he had some trouble with a window and his land-
lord told him that all subsequent repairs on
the building will have to be undertaken by the
tenants since the building is basically dere-
lict and he doesn't want to put any more money
into it. Richard has been married and he has
a pleasantly amicable relation with his ex-wife,
and with a lovely daughter that he's obviously
concerned with. But he's basically a loner. He
thinks of coming out here, looking around for
a house, but I sense it's going to be rather
hard for him to leave San Francisco where he
lives across from the big Sears Roebuck on
Geary. He's an old friend of Ron Loewinsohn's,
and again to my mind, his basic teaching comes
from Jack Spicer. He's a westerner. The first
time he'd ever been east I think was when he
was 35; he'd never been *east* of the Mississippi.
Richard told me one last lovely story:--when
he got to the Metropolitan Museum, he was
charmed by the fact that when he looked at all
the lovely Rembrandts his shadow was on the
paint. Which ain't ego, it just means wanting
to be counted too.

André: Another friend of yours who has sort of
entered the "pantheon" is Gary Snyder. Is he
around here?

Creeley: He lives up in Nevada City. Richard,
now, had been active in the Diggers Community,

the Free City and very much in the whole Haight-
Ashbury activity before the whole ugliness in-
vaded it. Gary, because of his formal background
in Zen, in Tibetan Buddhism particularly, feels
a more extensive responsibility to an educational process. He's not particularly interested in
teaching in formal institutions, he's very involved in ecological--I suppose we could call
them spiritual--states of being. He's just completed building in the last year a lovely house
in Japanese design up in the woods above Nevada
City. Richard actually will walk around the
city and people recognize him or dig him. People
want something else from Gary: they want to be
instructed, they want to be shown particular
disciplines. I don't think they ask that of
Richard. Gary's more in the situation of Allen
Ginsberg. A different use of it. I mean Allen
still stays, I think, like a lovely [pause]
rabbinical [pause] Buddhist.

[Unmuzzled Ox I:1,
November 1971]

Zee vapide — releasing

Thirty   rehearsing   )(different)
                                        view)

Dear Mr Creeley
Don't you make through definition or allusion
what is intimate
to you /
instead of working with
what is
intimate to
you
or is there some
give and
take between
the two.

$3.00